Mommy Reboot

A Busy Mom's Guide to Self-Care

By

Jody Agard

We ourselves feel that what we are doing is just a drop in the ocean. But the ocean would be less because of that missing drop.

—MOTHER TERESA

Cover photograph by Steph Jones Photography
StephJonesPhotography.com

Book design and production by Fiverr @Leahdesign

Editing by Philip Mygatt

Printed in the United States of America

First Printing: August 2018

Mommy Reboot ISBN-13: 978-1723368950

Dedication

To the busy mom who juggles a million details and then crashes on her bed from exhaustion...

This book is for you.

To the mom questioning if she's a good mom...

This book is for you.

To the mom falling apart...

This book is for you.

To the mom who feels selfish and an overwhelming sense of guilt every time she does anything for herself. ..

This book is for you.

To the mom so busy taking care of everyone else that she forgets to take care of herself...

This book is for you.

To the mom who cries herself to sleep at night with worry, fear, and frustration and then pulls up her big-girl panties and marches on for her kids and family...

This book is for you.

To the new mom who can't even describe the extent of her fatigue with words...

This book is for you.

To the mom who's on the verge of burn out and really just needs life to chill out a bit...

This book is for you.

You found this because you're looking for solutions. You're searching for something. Maybe it's a sense of relief, inner peace, or genuine happiness for your life. Or, maybe for the first time in your mom journey, you're finally beginning to understand the importance of taking care of yourself but you just want to know how in the world you'll find time to do that when your life is already so demanding. You'll get that and much more.

Now turn the page and keep reading.

XoXo,

Jody

Table of Contents

A Bit About Me

I think every mom's journeys starts with their own mom paving the way for them. It feels like each mom passes an invisible baton to their daughters and onto the next young generation of moms.

The good, the bad, and the ugly.

My mom was born in the 1950's. "Serving others" was what she was groomed for. She wasn't a stay-at-home mom like her own mom though; she was a full-time Registered Nurse. Growing up (and today), she's everything you could ask for in a mom. She's nurturing, loving, and always supportive. Even when she's been pissed at me, I've always known she loves me. Back in her mom hay day times, she was big on structure. I.e. strict bed times, homework, dinner at 5pm, etc. She ran a tight ship. Like most moms, even though she had her husband (my dad) by her side, she was the CEO of the house. My brother and I both knew who the one was running the show.

I was blessed to have one of the most loving dad's too. He was the guy who everyone waved at and would give you his shirt off his back. He was in the Navy in the early seventies and a carpenter by trade. He was more about the fun and living life; a free spirit.

Sadly, I only got to spend a short fifteen years with my dad; we lost him to suicide my freshman year of high school.

I can't even begin to describe with words how grief-stricken and devastated I was. My dad was my *everything*, and I was "his little girl". He had a way of making me feel special, and adored. I felt like he was the only one who really "got me". At the time, I was so much closer to him than I was my mom. She and I were more like oil and water; we never quite meshed.

I was absolutely beside myself when he died. Admittedly, I went through a dark phase of *"How could you leave me here with **her**?"*

It wasn't until I had my first child six years later when I realized just how blessed I really was. I finally began to appreciate the fact that I had been given the gift of learning the grace and wisdom only a mother could teach her daughter.

Her strength was woven into all aspects of her life. She taught me through her actions that to be a good mom, kids come first.

Always. Even at the expense of your *own* well-being sometimes.

This wasn't something that she sat down and explained to me. It was something I witnessed and later modeled. I didn't do this consciously, I just did it.

I wanted nothing more than to be a good mom the way she was to my brother and me. I admired the way she held three jobs, prepared good meals, always kept the house clean, kept us in private school, took us on family vacations, figured out ways to buy me my must-have designer jeans, and consistently showed us unconditional love that was laced beautifully with tough love. It was seemingly done so effortlessly too. (Ha! I know better now.)

Naturally, these are the things I worked towards when I had kids of my own. I followed right in her footsteps.

Well, ok – maybe not entirely.

I had my first son when I was twenty-one. I was a baby having a baby really. I got a changing table for my twenty-first birthday while all my friends were out slamming shots and partying for spring break.

When I was a little girl, I always pictured having the "happily ever-after" family. I'd find a stellar guy who was as awesome as my dad, we'd travel together, and then he'd ask my family's permission to propose to me which of course they'd give him a resounding YES! Then, he'd find some romantic, unexpected, magical way of asking me to take his hand in marriage, at which point I'd give him another resounding YES! Our parents (who were best buds by this point) would throw us a big engagement party, we'd get married at our fairytale wedding, go on an amazing honeymoon, come back, buy a house, and start banging out kids.

Yeah, zero of that happened. Like none of it.

What I *didn't* picture was having a kid out of wed-lock, and being a single mom by the time I was twenty-two.

Those were both very big no-no's in my middle class, Italian Catholic family.

But --- that's exactly what happened.

I knew my son came into my life for a reason though.

He was my angel disguised in a chubby eight-pound fourteen ounce, brown haired, brown-eyed costume.

I'm getting ahead of myself though…let me back up and fill you in on how I got there.

My best friend and I had gone out for the night, and we were both single. We had just arrived at our favorite nightclub so we were standing at the bar watching everyone dance when this guy walked up to me, grabbed my hand and pulled me out onto the dance floor. I was eighteen, living on my own for the first time (with my best-friend) and enrolled in college.

I fell head over heels for this guy. By the time I found out he was a drug dealer…it was too late. I didn't care. I was already in love with him.

Maybe you're thinking…middle-class, catholic school girl falls in love with her drug dealer?

Nope I myself had absolutely *no* interest in drugs. I was petrified of them actually.

But, I had *daddy issues*. (Duh, my dad who I adored died by suicide when I was fifteen.)

Anyway, back to my story. For unknown reasons, this guy's lifestyle intrigued me and I felt "safe" in his arms. I had no idea his way of living even existed. I felt like I had been living under a rock. For my eighteen-year old self though…being exposed to it was new and exciting.

{Rebellion at its finest.}

It was like something from the movies; he'd leave the house around midnight to go stand on the corner and deal drugs in the hood. Drugs as in, crack. Like crack cocaine. I had no idea these things happened outside Hollywood movies, much less in the city I lived. By the time he would return in the wee hours of the morning, I was up getting ready to head to work. I absolutely *adored* my job; I worked at an assisted living group home. The residents were wheelchair-bound cerebral palsy adults. I did everything from changing diapers, to bathing, to feeding, to changing out catheters, to taking them for walks outside. We called them "clients", but they felt more like family -- only I was being paid to take care of them.

I worked the morning shift so I had to be there at seven o'clock. Before walking out the door each morning, the boyfriend would often tell me some crazy story about a "crack head" he had to deal with. When I returned from work in the afternoon, my stories were usually along the lines of how "Paul" used his communication board and pointed to each letter to spell out that he loved me and never wanted me to leave. Or how for the first time "Rebecca" didn't throw her breakfast at me and even patted my hand as I fed her.

The worlds I was walking in and out of each day, were so completely opposite. Somehow though, I felt at home in each one.

At night I worked at a restaurant waiting tables, so I felt like we rarely saw each other. I was inside some sort of gangster love story movie nonetheless though. For Christmas one year he gave me a radio without the box and told me it didn't come with one. The kicker was, I believed him. So much so that I remember getting into an argument with my mom as I tried to defend him.

Over the years, she's tried to explain to me what she went through during that time, but I can't even fathom what that must've *really* been like. (She probably needs to write a book of her own.)

A couple years into this rendezvous with trouble, I got pregnant. Until now, I've never shared the following story with anyone but a select few of very close friends.

The pregnancy was accidentally on purpose. You see, the truth is, a couple months before getting pregnant the boyfriend started throwing away my birth control pills.

By the way, these were pills my mom was paying for because it was her "insurance" that I wouldn't get pregnant. Or so she thought anyway.

Well, he'd throw them away and somehow I thought it was "cute".

{I know.}

Honestly, there was a big part of me that never thought it would really happen. I knew I was playing with fire though. I also heard that it takes months for the body to get regulated after you go off the pills so I thought I'd at least have some buffer time. Nope. Not us. I stopped in May and I was pregnant by July.

I was shocked.

He was thrilled. He was "ready" for another baby. After all, he already had one of his own. (Did I forget to mention that?) His daughter was two years old when I met him. I absolutely fell in love with that child. Looking back, she was the first little human I ever mothered. Well, besides my "clients" at the group home of course.

I fell in love with my boyfriend even more once I saw him with his daughter. He was usually "Mr. Tough Guy", but the way he was with his daughter made my heart melt. He treated her like a princess when she was around. The custody him and his ex-girlfriend had was pretty flexible. It seemed as though she'd let him have his daughter any weekend he wanted. So he'd take her often. Once I came into the picture, it was easy for him to run off in the streets because I loved watching her. So this beautiful little child and I would spend lots and lots of time together. There were weekends when that's all I really wanted to do, just hanging out with her. I became friendly with his ex-so sometimes I would bypass my boyfriend and ask the mom directly if I could take her to the park or the movies or do something fun.

Even though I had this "practice" of mothering, I was still scared shitless. I knew I was in way over my head and I had **no** business having a child of my own. I also knew I had no other choice though.

I remember calling my mom before my 11am shift to tell her the news. I called her from the payphone near the bathrooms of the Italian restaurant I was working. My hands were shaking out of control. I kept repeating *"I can't do this!"* My best friend who also worked with me stood beside me, encouraging me.

"Just do it. You have to Jody."

{Ok, here it goes.}

"Hey, Mom."

"Hi, Honey. How are you?"

"I'm gooooood. How are you?"

"What's up? Are you ok?"

"Yeah, I'm fine. But I do have something to tell you."

"Ok?"

I must have paused a bit too long.

"Jody? What is it?"

Her mommy spidey senses must have kicked in.

"Jody? Whaaat? What's wrong? You're not pregnant are you?"

My heart raced, my palms got sweaty and I wanted to run. *"Yeah, I am."*

She was quiet only for a moment but her disappointment was louder than ever. *"Oh Jody. What are you going to do?"*

*"What do you mean **what am I going to do**? I'm keeping it!"*

There were no other options in my mind. I knew I just had to *"figure it out"*.

My mom told me years later that when she hung up the phone, she burst into tears and cried nonstop for three days.

Dating this guy was bad enough, but having a child with him was my mom's worst fear. Once the initial shock wore off, she embraced the idea of becoming a grandmother though. Just two weeks later we met for lunch. I'll never forget the relief I felt as she handed me a baby bag with a beautiful card and a cute little onesie inside. She reminded me that she'd always be there to help me. In that moment I felt her disappointment was replaced with acceptance and excitement. Her loving support made me feel slightly less of a "fuck-up".

Five months into the pregnancy and on Thanksgiving weekend the boyfriend and I broke up. It was a mutual decision but I really didn't know where I was going to live. Either go back to my mom's house and be around my toxic stepfather, or be homeless.

Needless to say, I reluctantly moved back home with my mom & stepdad, about two hours away from my ex.

My mom on the other hand, was thrilled. She fed me good meals, came to every doctor's appointment with me, and we went to every single Lamaze class together. We had some of the most heartfelt, mother-daughter conversations we've ever had and we bonded in ways I never knew possible.

I worked at a local grocery store just a couple miles down the road and since my ex "needed" the one car we had, I left it with him and rode my bike to work.

At my thirty-eight-week check-up, my mid-wife asked *"What do you do for exercise?"* I casually answered *"I ride my bike to work."*

"Your <u>bike</u>?"

"Yeah. A bicycle."

"Ok, you can't do that anymore. If you lose your balance and fall you could really hurt yourself, or the baby."

So if I didn't get a ride from my mom, I waddled my thirty-nine week ass back and forth.

A week later my boss pulled me aside *"You know your due date is almost here, I think it's really time you go home to rest."*

Translation: You're a liability. If your water breaks, and you slip, we don't want to get sued.

I remained in contact with the ex-boyfriend for the entire six months we were apart. He'd call to ask about my doctor's appointments and the progress of the baby.

Just a few days before giving birth, he reappeared. He wanted to move in together and give it another shot. "He wanted his family back." I still believed I could have that happily-ever family so that was all it took for me.

We found a place and after a tsunami sized argument with my mom, I moved out just days before I gave birth. Initiated by step-dad, they made me sign a contract stating that if I left, I was never allowed to move back in again.

A week past my due date and at five o'clock on a Thursday morning in April I woke up from a dead sleep with contractions. With disgust politely pushed aside and the excitement of my son's arrival, my mom and the boyfriend were both there beside me at the hospital. We were one big happy family. Actually it went well. Each respected the other's space, and they played nice. They even ordered Chinese food together and the smell of it made me want to punch them both.

After sixteen hours of induced (back) labor, two and a half hours of hardcore pushing, and a natural childbirth, my beautiful son finally made his appearance.

In my immature twenty-one-year-old brain, I really thought that having a baby would shape the boyfriend up and he'd stop dealing drugs. I clung to the hope that he'd want to adopt a healthier family lifestyle.

I can only laugh at the insanity of that now.

For the first few months he did, but the novelty quickly wore off.

Needless to say, once I became a mommy things got old real quick.

Being a twenty-one-year-old girl making bad decisions was one thing, but being a mom making bad decisions was another.

I'll never forget my first big "aha" moment.

It was a Friday, about six in the morning. I had been up all night waiting for him to come home. I hadn't heard from him for hours. I didn't know if something had gone bad and he was lying dead somewhere, or if he was cheating on me. I tried getting a hold of him but he didn't return my calls. I was worried sick. All of these crazy thoughts and visions spun through my mind. I was also pissed. I thought *"What if something was wrong with our son and we were at the hospital?"* As I sat on our balcony off of our bedroom watching the sun come up, I realized I shouldn't be having these worries. I saw for the first time the *insanity* of the lifestyle I was living.

What the fuck am I doing?

How did I get here?

I don't belong here.

I deserve better.

This isn't about me anymore; this is about my son!

I thought about leaving the boyfriend before, but I couldn't. I had no idea how I would survive financially with a child. I felt trapped.

However, on this morning none of that mattered. I didn't care if we ended up homeless. I'd have to find a way to just figure it out.

And I did.

By this time, my son was eighteen-months old, and there I was – a single mom.

I know.

Shocker right?

I really had no idea what I was doing.

I poured every ounce of love I could into this child though.

The only thing that I knew for sure was that I loved my kid so much and I wanted to give him the best life I possibly could; regardless of the choices I had previously made.

I knew every decision I made moving forward would directly affect my son. So I made a pact with myself that I would only make decisions that would ultimately benefit him, no matter how hard they were on me.

The commitment to want to better myself was so great that it scared me to death.

There I was, deep in the trenches of motherhood; clueless, afraid, and already feeling like a failure.

I was still working full-time but money was tight. I wasn't getting any child support so most of the time I felt like I was working just to pay for daycare.

I wasn't only learning to navigate the ins and outs of being a new mom, I was also forced to learn about the difficulties in raising a bi-racial child in a still somewhat prejudice world. The first time I ever experienced it was at a Wal-Mart. I proudly had my tanned skinned chubby baby sitting in the front section of the cart. I was making funny faces to make him laugh as we passed a couple in the jewelry section. The husband turned to the wife and said *"What a waste of a beautiful white woman; such a disgrace."*

Once again, I never knew such a thing existed. I mean, we studied it in school and I heard about it on the news, but as a "white girl" I never personally experienced such a thing. I guess I was too naïve to think we'd ever have to experience it either. For the first time in my mom journey, I also experienced "the mama bear syndrome."

My blood boiled. The mama bear in me wanted to tackle the couple to the ground and tell them both to fuck off. I was too shocked and distraught to turn around and say anything though.

His father still lived a couple hours away. He'd make attempts to come and see him but they never quite panned out. Something would always come up. Every time I said "your daddy's coming" my then toddler son would run into his room, grab his suitcase that was bigger than him and he'd wait by the front door. For hours.

After several traumatic episodes of me peeling my screaming son away from the door, I finally learned to not even tell him if he was coming.

By the time my son was three-years old his dad finally agreed to officially terminate his parental rights.

I was legally his only parent. To me, the documents, the hearing, and the entire legal process were just a formality; I had been his only parent for a year and half before that.

My son (Derrick) and I lived in a cute little two-bedroom duplex near great schools and just three miles down the road from my mom. By this time, I was living the nine-to-five office life working at a large home builder and land title real estate office. I quickly started making my way up the ladder.

I stayed away from the dating scene and just focused on figuring out this whole mommying thing.

We found our new norm, and life was good.

--Fast Forward a Few Years--

When my son was five I met a guy who really caught my attention.

Not at a night club and he wasn't a drug dealer either. This time, at a convenient store...I was cashing in a winning scratch off ticket and he was in line to pay for his gas and grab a banana. He was a Land Surveyor with a pressure washing side hustle business.

My family called him a "prince". Everyone loved him. So did I. (As much as I could back then.)

This was new territory for me, dating with a child.

I had gone on a few dates over the years, but nothing ever serious. I'd usually start off by telling my date, *"I have six kids"* and just as their mouth dropped; I'd say *"just kidding." I have a son, and he's half black. So if you have a problem with that, you should tell me now."*

Most I never heard from again. That was good in my eyes. I didn't have time for games. I was very protective.

This guy though, he seemed to embrace it all. I still waited a few months before I let him meet my son though.

When they finally did meet, they had an *instantaneous* bond. I can't really put it into words, but it was beautifully remarkable.

We got married a year later and had a traditional Italian wedding with nearly two-hundred guests. It was beautiful.

Just months after the wedding, he made it official and adopted my son. We had another huge party to celebrate with all of our closest friends and relatives.

Within a year and all part of our beautiful little plan, I got pregnant. This time, I couldn't wait to tell my mom. We were all thrilled that our little family was growing.

He came to every doctor's appointment, he wouldn't let me lift heavy things, and he doted over me non-stop. It actually got kind of annoying.

This was why I knew something was up when my husband was nowhere to be found on the weekend we moved into our beautiful brand new home.

I was four months pregnant and we had gotten into an argument on a Friday night. He left mad and said he was going out for a while. He never did that, so I assumed he just went fishing. When he didn't come home I assumed he went to his mom's house so I wasn't worried. I figured I'd just let him blow off some steam.

When I talked to him on Saturday he said he was out fishing all night and he had to go into the office to do some work for a bit. I was pissed he left me to unpack the house by myself but I fully trusted him. By Sunday, I was still unloading boxes, putting away dishes, and setting up our new house; with my mom, step-dad, and six year old son. At this point my eyebrows were raised; it was so unlike him. But he swore nothing happened and he was just at his family's house, working, and fishing.

My intuition told me otherwise so I just kept following it. Within a week, I was on the phone with the girl he met at a bar on Friday night.

Thanks to my pregnancy I was up several times a night having to go pee. On one random bathroom trip, I heard a noise coming from the garage. "Ding." I kept hearing it. So I followed it out to the garage, opened my husband's truck door and found his text messages going off.

{Why in the #@$* is his phone in the truck!?}

I dreadfully read the first one "I miss you sunshine." Shaking, I blocked the number I was calling from and called back the number. A woman's voice answered "Hello?" I hung up.

Sobbing, I sat up all night thinking about what I

what I was going to do. I had my plan.

I wiped my eyes and as the sun rose, I proceeded like any other morning. I got my son up and ready for school, I made breakfast and I anxiously waited for them to leave for the day. At eight o'clock I kissed them goodbye as they headed out the door.

I watched as they drove away.

I knew my husband would be at work all day, but I wanted to get this over with. My hands were shaking as I dialed back the woman's number.

She answered, "Hello?"

"Hi. My name is Jody, I was wondering, do you know a {first and last name of my husband}?"

"Hmmm, no. Maybe my husband does though?"

I pleaded, "Listen. He's my husband. We haven't even been married a full year yet, he recently adopted my son, I'm four months pregnant with his child and I feel in my heart he's been cheating with you. Please, from woman to woman just tell me the truth."

She paused, and then burst into tears.

She wasn't really married; she said that out of shock. She was actually divorced because her husband had cheated on her.

As I sat on our new couch listening to the *gory*

details of their weekend together, my heart shattered. She had *no* idea he was married. It was as though I, and the life we built never even existed.

I had held him and our marriage on such a high pedestal but that all came crashing down.

I felt like he had ripped my heart out of my chest, threw it on the ground and smashed it like an old cigarette.

I was beyond heartbroken.

We tried to work it out for the sake of the kids, but I just couldn't. The damage was done.

I couldn't even look him in the eyes, let alone be intimate with him. I had lost **all** respect for him.

We were divorced by the time my youngest was ten-months old.

THIS was *not* part of my plan.

There were no words to describe the pain and anger I felt towards my ex. I was devastated for my own reasons, but I was downright irate that he had robbed our boys of security and a family life. Especially for my oldest who has been down this road before. I trusted him, and I deeply regretted it.

I was extremely resentful towards him in those days.

But – life went on.

In the big picture, getting through my divorce was small potatoes compared to getting through my dad's suicide though. I always reminded myself of that. If I was able to get through the single most traumatic time of my life, I could get through the divorce.

Plus, in the aftermath of losing my dad at such a young age I ended up adopting the belief that everything happened for a reason. There's always a bigger picture, and a much bigger plan in the works. Even though it was painful and I couldn't understand it, I knew this to be true from the core of my being.

Later, I realized that our brief marriage really wasn't about my husband and me; his purpose for coming into my life was to give my oldest son a dad and to bring our youngest into the world. He's remained very active in both the boys' lives, and for that I am beyond grateful. My oldest is now twenty-years old and they still carry that same bond today. As for him and I, we've become good friends again.

So, with a ten-month-old and a seven-year-old in tow, I was back to being a single mom; only now I had *two* kids instead of one.

Eventually, we found yet *another* new norm and created our own version of a family life with just the three of us.

2010 –

The Year Everything Changed

My boys were now twelve and five years old. It was quite the crazy ride, but thankfully, I made it through the deep trenches of mommyhood.

But, as I advanced from a newbie mom to a seasoned mom, there was something inside me that yearned for more.

Even though I had a good career, I wanted to become more of myself.

If I'm being honest, the words *"My kids are my everything."* never really resonated with me. Because of that, I thought for a long time something was wrong with me. So I kept it to myself.

I felt ashamed for thinking it and wondered if I was a bad mom for not feeling the same way "most moms did".

I loved being a mom, but I also desperately wanted to still be <u>me</u>.

The only problem I had was that I didn't know exactly who I was beyond the titles behind my name; i.e. Mom, daughter, employee. Somewhere deep down I knew I was in there though.

Before I even became a mom, so many "well-seasoned" moms - all with good intentions, would tell me things like *"Once you have kids, your life is over."*

They'd add...

"No more uncomplicated dates."

"No traveling."

"No more lunches with your girlfriends."

"Every ounce of energy will go into your kids."

"Get ready to not have a life anymore."

"You can forget about sleep."

"Your body is never going to be the same once you have kids."

Great, sign me up.

I bought into all these things for years and just accepted it as "that's what motherhood is all about".

Sacrifice.

Sacrifice.

Sacrifice.

I thought the best way to serve my kids and my family was to always put *their* needs before my own.

So I did that.

I ran myself into the ground doing it too.

There was always this underlying feeling that I needed to be doing *something*, <u>anything</u>. Sitting still was never an option. If I tried to sit for a minute, it felt so weird and uncomfortable. I felt like I was ready to jump out of my own skin.

It was bad.

I even struggled when I would snuggle up on the couch with my kids to watch a movie. It took everything I had in me to stay there for the entire movie. Half way through it, sometimes I would get up and start doing things until one of my kids would tell me to come and sit.

I'd have to force myself to be present for my boys. Even when I'd rock them in the glider, I had to fight the pull to go clean the kitchen or start a load of laundry. *"I don't have time to sit!"*

Clearly, I had it all backwards.

This on-the-go mentality worked for a while; until it didn't anymore.

In December of 2010 I had reached my breaking point.

I was still working at a title company office and had been for most of my adult years.

My boys were in sixth grade and kindergarten. I was still a single mom. I had been dating a guy named Josh for two years (who's now my wonderful hubby) but we weren't living together yet.

After dinner one night I was washing the pots and pans and I heard myself yelling at the kids.

Readjusting my voice from a calm, yet stern tone to one where I'm yelling usually took a while.

This was different though.

I <u>really</u> heard myself this time. I was like *"Wow! That was bitchy."*

It hit me hard. So I rewound 15 minutes, and then an hour, and then a day, and then a week, and then a month. And when I did that, I was like *"Holy shit! Who am I becoming? Since when did my fuse get so short?"*

It honestly scared me. I didn't want to be that mom who was always screaming at her kids because she was one big ball of stress.

I was generally a happy, positive person; the girl who was always lifting others up and finding a way to find humor in most everything. I could laugh and make some sort of sarcastic joke about almost anything. Not much brought me down.

I realized I was being extra bitchy, one hundred times less patient, and I was getting irritated about pretty much everything though.

Everyone (and everything) got on my nerves.

It didn't matter what they were doing. Even strangers started to annoy me.

"I don't want to be this person." I thought.

I realized I was exhausted, not just physically but *mentally* too. I was tired of being tired. I was sick of not feeling fulfilled. I craved more. I longed to wake up with meaning, and to feel excited about my day. There wasn't anything I wouldn't do for my kids, but I wanted to feel I had a purpose beyond being a mom. My kids were the best thing that happened to me, but I also felt like I had lost myself somewhere in raising them. I wanted to not feel so overwhelmed and I begged for inner peace.

I felt like every day was a struggle to keep my head above water.

That moment at the sink was the beginning of my transformational, soul searching journey.

And it wasn't pretty, or *easy*.

When I took a step back, I saw that the moment I lost my dad to suicide when I was fifteen years old --- the "running" began.

This running, showed up as busyness. Well, it also

showed up in my relationships too…but that's a whole other book.

I was running from the deep pain within by keeping myself busy enough so I wouldn't have time to think. Somewhere deep inside, I knew that if I had time for thought, then I would think about the hardships of my life. The pain of losing my dad and going through a divorce was too great for me to bear. So I became "Queen Busy Body". I was good at it too.

I mean, I was *really* good. My boss loved it. I always stayed as late as I could and I was there early in the mornings. Most of the time, I didn't take my lunch either. I always went above and beyond, so I worked my way up to the top pretty quickly. My house was clean. I was always doing something with the kids. I never stopped.

It wasn't until I started doing some honest soul searching when I realized just how empty I felt inside. I felt depleted, like I had nothing left to give.

On the outside, I was "skinny" but certainly not healthy. I was smoking a pack of cigarettes a day and if I did eat, it was anything I could get my hands on and filled with empty calories. Most of the time I ate on-the-go too; at my desk, in the car, or standing up.

"I had too many things to do; I didn't have time to sit."

When I'd clock out from my full-time job, I'd

throw my "mom hat" on and race to grab my kids from daycare and afterschool.

I had to make it there by 6 PM (to avoid a late charge and the walk of shame to be the last one to pick up my kids.)

Once we were home, I'd race to make dinner; still in my heels and office clothes.

While I cooked dinner I had the boys sitting at the breakfast bar in front of me so I could simultaneously help them with their homework.

Once dinner was ready, we'd all race over to the table to eat together.

After dinner, I was practically pushing them into the showers so I could start cleaning up the kitchen.

First my oldest, then my youngest.

My nightly goal was to have everything cleaned up by the time they came out because that was our time to hang out and spend some quality time together.

We'd either watch a movie or one of their favorite TV shows. Sometimes we'd read, or play a game, other times we'd go for a short walk.

By the time we got settled, it was usually seven o'clock. If everything went according to plan, I knew I had exactly one hour before I had to activate *the bed time plan.*

Most of the time I was anxiously waiting to "clock out". (As if moms really ever do that.)

Mom truth: On some nights I was so exhausted, I'd lie about the time and said it was later than it really was.

"Oh boys! Look at the time! It's already eight o'clock! Hurry, let's get in bed."

But really, it was only seven-thirty.

When it came to our night-time routine, I was like a robot.

I did this day in and day out for years, like clockwork.

At the end of the night when the boys were in bed, I finally had my "me-time".

The idea of reading a good book or taking a hot bubble bath sounded good on paper. Most of the time I was too tired to do anything other than just pass out with my makeup still caked onto my eyeballs though.

My 5:30 alarm would go off and I'd do it all over again.

While I was standing at the kitchen sink that one particular evening, I realized how sick and tired I was of living that way.

I was tired of putting myself at the bottom of my mile-long to-do list.

Hell, who was I kidding? Most of the time I didn't even make it on my to-do list.

I was tired of not being able to fully enjoy my kids.

I felt like I constantly had to have my "game face" on but I didn't have the energy to put it on anymore. In fact, I think I just wanted to put my "game face" away for a while.

I wanted more.

I wanted time to breathe.

Time to read if I wanted to.

Time to reflect.

Time to just be ME.

I wanted to feel excited about my day!

To feel I had a purpose, and a life outside of my kids.

I struggled.

I wanted to feel alive.

I wanted to feel un-rushed for once. I was always

hurrying.

I wanted to feel connected to myself.

I wanted to feel more present with my kids.

I wanted to feel **whole**.

For the few times I actually did do something for myself, I wanted to stop feeling the insane amount of perpetual mom guilt. ("Feeling bad" took on a whole new meaning after I had kids. And it seemed to worsen over the years.)

But, I had no idea what this all meant, nor how to "get" any of it. All I knew was that I was desperate for something <u>different</u>.

On the outside, it appeared I had it all too.

I was just promoted at work and offered a position I had been working towards my entire career.

The kicker was though, I didn't want it.

My heart was opening and I wanted to write books and start my own life-coaching practice instead. I felt a strong tug at my heart to help in bigger ways.

I had two healthy kids.

I had a loving boyfriend who adored me and my kids. I had an ex-husband who was in the boy's life and we were successfully co-parenting (most of the time).

I had a beautiful four-bedroom home with a pool.

I had a good support team: my mom and a great circle of friends.

But it didn't matter.

I craved more.

Something deeper.

I really just wanted to wake up feeling alive I guess. I wanted to feel as though I was actually thriving instead of merely surviving.

And by the way, I felt *awful* for wanting more. (There's that guilt monster again.)

I knew there were others who had less than me, so I felt like a spoiled little brat for wanting more.

Who was I for wanting more?

I was tired of living the way I was and I knew I needed change though.

I had absolutely no clue where to start. Well, I did know two things.

1. I had to take better care of myself.

2. I had to figure out a way to put myself first and nurture myself the way I so easily nurtured

my kids…and without my mothering suffering too.

This is where my self-care journey began.

At this point, I had zero clues what self-care was, how it applied to me, or how I was even going to fit it into my busy schedule.

At the time, my form of self-care was taking showers, brushing my teeth, and getting my hair and nails done every once in a while.

I was a busy mom so I had no idea what that "plan" would look like yet. All I knew was that I needed it to be practical so it could fit into my chaotic life.

At first, I just played around with self-care. I started allowing myself to have more fun and relax more. I began releasing guilt and learned how to be gentle and forgiving towards myself.

I started becoming more aware of my inner chatter.

{That was frightening!}

I learned how to be more loving towards myself and I stopped putting unrealistic expectations on myself. I also started to let go of the perfectionist in me.

I started to care less about what other people

thought and more about how *I* felt.

I began sprinkling self-care into my day. Small at first, but as the days went on I would *up* the antics and challenge myself a bit more.

I started seeing results and my life was *rapidly* improving.

Within months, I stopped smoking, started writing my book *"Let Love in 101; A Practical Guide to Love and Happiness"*, left my comfortable paying full-time land title office job to take the leap into entrepreneurship, started my own coaching practice, and even started eating better.

That book later became a best-seller and I found myself doing speaking engagements and radio interviews.

My life looked NOTHING like it once did.

And it's all because I cared enough to take care of *myself* for once.

I eventually learned that taking care of ME *is* a part of taking care of my kids. It's the bridge to better taking care of my family. Self-care made me an even **better** mom.

I taught myself how to fill up my cup first and use that proverbial oxygen mask on myself, and I was reaping the rewards.

I began adopting the belief that in fact; the best way to serve anyone was to put myself *first*!

{Gasp!}

I started to believe I didn't have to choose my kids over myself and that I **could** "HAVE IT ALL". I began to understand that I didn't need to change any of my circumstances either.

All it took was a commitment, some pivots in my thinking and small daily actions.

Being a mom can be *really* hard.

Damn can it be hard! The things I do for my kids day in and day out often go unnoticed and unappreciated.

But beneath all the crap that motherhood sometimes brings, I have unconditional love for my kids that drives me to be better than I was yesterday.

I have no doubt it's the same with you.

Being a better mom means allowing my own needs to come before my family's sometimes.

I no longer wait to try to squeeze self-care into my day. Instead, I build my day *around* my self-care practice.

For example, today I'm going to my favorite acai bowl place and then taking a stroll around my favorite lake for my self-care. I scheduled shuttling my youngest to his friend's house around it because it was already my self-care was already in my calendar.

I do it because I know self-care reboots me. Think about your laptop or computer for a second. Has it ever ran super slow or even froze so you were forced to shut it down? When you started it back up again, you probably found it to run way quicker and more efficiently, right?

That's what self-care does for moms. That pause, that activity, the thing you do to take care of yourself gives you the jumpstart you need to keep all systems running smoothly.

Because of my own commitment to self-care my relationships are better, my parenting is better, and the way I view struggles is better. I have the stamina, clarity, and mental energy to get through the days that aren't always so easy too.

It hasn't been easy though. Self-care is like anything else that's new. It takes tons of practice and lots of patience.

When I finally stopped feeling ashamed for the way I was feeling (wanting more, etc.), I shared my feelings with my besties and other mom friends. A funny thing happened... I realized I wasn't alone.

Come to find out, moms all over the globe felt

similar to the way I did in one way or another.

It's funny how when you're going through the mud of mommyhood you feel alienated and think you're in it all by yourself. *"Nobody understands what I'm going through"* we cry!

When in fact we **all** get it! Like - we <u>*REALLY*</u> get it.

Motherhood is just another name for sisterhood.

I wrote this book for you sister. We're on this journey together, and I'm really happy you found your way to me.

By the way, speaking of a sisterhood -- you are cordially invited to join our private **Mommy Reboot Facebook tribe**! It's filled with busy, down-to-earth, non-judgey, compassionate moms like yourself who are committed to being a good mom by taking care of themselves. We're all just trying to figure out this whole mommying thing, and we get to do it together. Come join us → **<u>facebook.com/groups/mommyreboot</u>** we'd love to have you!

<u>How This Book Works:</u>

Stay committed, it's a practice.

Most of the chapters are intentionally short.

After some chapters you'll see a "Now What?" section. This area will help to tie it all in. I'll give you direct action steps and ways to apply what I previously went over.

Once you read the book from cover to cover, keep it around for a bit. You'll likely find that you need reminders along the way and long after you've finished the book. The principles you learn won't all be learned overnight. It might take time for some of them to really "click". I suggest when you need an extra boost, pick up the book, close your eyes and open to a random page. I have no doubt that you'll be led right back to the words you needed to hear the most.

Let this book be the ONE thing you do every day for self-care. As you're about to learn, my goal is to make the art of good self-care *uncomplicated*. Reading just _one_ page each day will surely get you on your way to practicing daily self-care. If you follow this book to the T, and in your own special way, I promise your life will improve drastically. And if your life is already pretty awesome, it'll make it even more kick ass!

Onward...

Motherhood in a Nutshell

"You cannot serve from an empty vessel."

~ Eleanor Brownn

Before motherhood...

I can't wait to be a mom. To have kids and snuggle them will be a dream come true. To watch them grow will be so amazing. I can't wait for that day.

Pregnancy...

I can't wait to wrap my arms around my baby. I can't even imagine how much I'm going to love him/her. The love I have for this child is already insane, so I can't even envision what it'll be like when I hold him/her in my arms! Just get here already!

The day you give birth...

I am so in love! The love I feel for my kid is indescribable and overwhelming. I love him/her so much it hurts. I never knew love like this. I didn't even think I was capable of loving another human this much. She/he is perfect and beautiful.

A few months in...

All this thing does is eat, sleep and poop. I never even knew the human body could be this tired. How can I be this exhausted and elated at the same time? I must be delirious.

Toddlers...

What the hell did I get myself into? I'm not fit to be a mom. I can't even go pee without this kid finding me. Can I just get some PEACE AND QUIET?! AND A MOMENT TO MYSELF MAYBE? I feel like all I do is chase this kid around. Every day we survive is a successful day. Man do I freaking love this kid though. I'm in awe at how he/she explores the world.

School aged kids...

My baby is growing up too fast. It seems like yesterday that I gave birth. Where does the time go? {Sigh}

Middle School...

What the? Where's my kid? What have you done with him? Who does she think she is?

High-school...

Can I put this kid back where it came from please? Military school? Boarding school? If she says "I **know** mom one more time..."! And the attitude...I don't deserve an attitude; I'm just trying to help!

Motherhood, and the way we mother our children is *constantly* changing and evolving. Once we have the infant thing figured out, there's the toddler tantrum thing and then the preschool phase.

Then comes elementary school--bringing on a whole new set of challenges and ways of handling our wee little ones.

Then comes middle school and high-school - kiss everything that worked in their younger year's *goodbye*.

Before we know it, parenting a young adult comes into play. Even though the child might be out of the house...the way you feel, the amount of love, the worry and the natural instinct to nurture **never** ceases, it only changes.

My oldest, now twenty-years-old is still learning about life. He's in the midst of figuring out who he is, where he belongs, and who he wants to become. He endures all the struggles that being a young adult brings.

"They say" that it's at this stage of parenting you just have to face the fact that the molding is already done. All you can do now is hope for the best and pray that all that you've taught them will be a constant voice in the back of their head as they walk through adulthood.

When I look back at mothering my own kids, I can clearly see that I've gone from worrying about my boys choking on small objects, to drowning in a pool, and then to worrying if they'll get caught up in peer pressure.

I've shed plenty of tears over the years, feeling overwhelmed and fearing I was epically failing at this thing called motherhood.

I've tried hard to do all the things that good moms do; give them tons of love, develop and maintain a healthy routine, tuck them in and read stories before bed, teach them the art of good manners and just being a kind human.

The list goes on and on and on.

It hasn't been easy that's for sure.

It took me ten years of being a mom to realize that while all the things I tried to instill in my kids were in fact important…it wasn't everything.

For me, the most important thing I want to teach my kids - by example – is that in order to live life to the fullest, it's not so much about the things we *do* in this world, its how we *feel,* and how we show up every day.

It's really all about our mindset and developing a healthy mental attitude towards life.

And in order to have a healthy mindset, we need time to breathe and reconnect with ourselves.

In order to be a good mom, I knew I had to feel

whole and take care of myself. I had to learn how to put myself first more consistently.

Its then, and only then, that I would be able to wholeheartedly take care of everyone else around me.

For me, this meant doing the things I loved; writing, meditating, being in nature, moving my body in ways I enjoyed, and to actually sit down to eat my meals instead of shoveling food in my mouth like our dog Peanut who doesn't think he's ever going to eat another meal again.

It meant that sometimes I would let the laundry sit there if I was tired because I knew that my sleep was way more important than any amount of laundry piling up. It meant that I would do things I enjoyed *regularly*.

The way I see it is that taking care of ourselves is a huge part of taking care of our kids.

They're not separate, they're a package deal. We can no longer afford to not take care of ourselves from the inside out. Life is too demanding and it'll chew us up and spit us out without some form of daily self-care.

Self-care isn't a luxury; it's our **duty** as modern day moms. We have to feel good and take care of ourselves to be the best moms we can be. We're at the helm of this ship, and if we go down everyone goes down.

The Basics Of

Self-Care

How Do I Know I Need Self-Care?

The short answer is: When you're mentally and emotionally *exhausted*.

We will go to the ends of the earth for our kids but no matter how much we love them - let's face it - being a mom can be grueling work.

So in truth, we need self-care every single day.

There are times in our lives however, when everything may feel like its "extra stressful". It might feel like things are spinning out of control and it's seemingly impossible to keep up. Those small, usually insignificant things suddenly become super annoying and we may find ourselves snapping at others when they've done nothing wrong.

These are red flags and a clear indication you need more self-care in your life.

Here's a list of some warning signs that you may be on the verge of mental and emotional exhaustion:

- You're easily irritated

- You're having anxiety attacks

- You can't sleep

- You lack motivation

- You feel numb or detached to the world around you

- You feel an urge to cry

- Small things upset you

- You feel nauseous and dizzy

None of these things should ever be ignored. There's no reason to feel ashamed about being so stressed out either.

Now is the time to take care of yourself and give your body what it's so badly craving. Rest, recharge, and reboot.

What is Self-Care?

One night, my husband and I were on a much needed date. We were sitting at the bar enjoying our happy hour cocktail and I started chatting with the lady next to me. I'd say she was probably in her late sixties.

She asked *"What do you do for work?"*

"I'm an author and self-care coach for busy moms." I replied.

"How fascinating! Self-care is so important. I don't know how moms nowadays do it with so many distractions. It was so different when I was raising my kids." She exclaimed.

"That's exactly why I'm so passionate about the work I do. Self-care has really transformed me and changed the way I show up as a mom to my kids. I think it's so important to teach the art of self-care for the modern mom and just learning what a self-care practice means to her."

She agreed. *"Yeah, I have a self-care practice too."*

"You do? That's awesome! If you don't mind me asking, what's your practice?" I asked.

"Oh, I wake up and I shower. Then I immediately put on my makeup. It doesn't matter whether I'm leaving the

house or not, I always iron my clothes and get dressed. After that I put curlers in my hair. I believe smelling good for my husband is really important so I always end my practice with a fragrant perfume."

At first, I wanted to jump up on the bar and scream for the whole place to hear *"Nooooooo! That is not self-care! There's so much more to it than that!!!"*

Then I remembered… <u>everyone</u> has their own practice. If those things make this woman feel good about herself, then who am I to say it's not enough?

At the end of the day, there is no right or wrong answer when it comes to defining self-care.

The definition from Webster's Dictionary is this...

Noun

Care for oneself.

Yep, that's it. Self-care is reduced to a measly three words that have absolutely no *real* meaning.

Thanks Webster, that explains everything.

If you ask a doctor what self-care is, you may get a different answer than if you asked a scientist or a therapist.

Defining self-care is a very personal thing.

It's like picking out a bra.

Someone else could *technically* do it for you, but it's so much better if you do it yourself.

Self-care refers to activities and practices that we can do on a *regular* basis to help reduce stress and maintain our whole well-being; our mind, body, **and** our soul.

Self-care isn't defined once.

You may have figured out what self-care was in your twenties (even if you didn't consciously define it) but now in your thirties, maybe you have no idea what it is.

The self-care practice for the woman with no kids versus the woman with kids is going to look completely different too.

Self-care is one of those things that's defined and then redefined again and again as you reach different phases of your life.

The practice of self-care, is always evolving.

The two-words 'self-care' leaves tons of room for interpretation here.

This is why it's so important to come up with your *own* definition, your own version of self-care. Only you can figure out what practicing self-care means to **you**.

To help you come up with your own definition,

here's what it is to me...

Self-care is a daily practice and one that will progress over time.

It's a decision, a discipline.

A choice to put my needs above everyone else's more often.

Self-care is about creating the space for me to take care of **me**.

It's about allowing myself to take some time to do some of the activities that I love and that feed my soul (like writing). It's not about feeling guilty either. I give myself permission to focus on me in any given moment.

To me, self-care is about deliberately doing something to take care of my mind, body, and soul

Self-care is about loving on and nurturing me.

It's about self-soothing myself back into a good mood the same way I would offer encouraging words to my kids.

It's about grace and forward progression, not perfection.

Self-care is about always being there for me.

It's about saying <u>no</u> to things I don't want to do so

I can say yes to my dreams and more things I <u>want</u> to do.

Self-care is an investment of time.

It's about saying <u>yes</u> often to the things that give me life, and fill me up.

It's about pinpointing my own needs and taking steps to meet them.

Self-care is about thoughtfully and purposely designing a life I don't need to escape from.

It's about doing what it takes to properly care for myself.

It's about talking to and treating myself as kindly as I would a friend, a loved one, or even a stranger.

It's an inner knowing that I am deserving of these things.

Self-care is the bridge to self-love.

It's about doing small daily things. Maybe it's a five-minute morning meditation or a fifteen-minute yoga routine on YouTube. Maybe the next week it's taking a nice hot bubble bath every night before bed.

Self-care can be whatever I want it to be and it doesn't have to be this huge burden or another item on my to-do list. But no matter what that "thing' is that

I'm doing, it must bring me joy, calm me down, or uplift me.

That's basically it in a nutshell.

What Self-Care is NOT...

It's equally important, if not maybe even **more** important to go over what self-care is **not**.

I think you might get the picture by now that self-care isn't about just brushing your teeth and having your hair and nails done every once in a while. Self-care isn't about lunches with your mom friends and girlfriends every six months either. It's not about the occasional spa day and it's certainly not about neglecting your family and your responsibilities either.

Self-care is not selfish.

It doesn't take away time from family/friends (it adds value).

It's not a one-time thing.

It is not lazy.

It's not an opportunity to feel guilty.

What's Me-Time?

When I first ask the moms I coach *"Do you get any me-time?"* They usually scoff, laugh or straight up say *"I WISH!"*

The words "Me-time" and "Moms" don't usually go hand-in-hand. But it needs to.

The definition of me time for the busy mom boils down to this: *That small window of time you get to spend **any** way you want.*

Me-time is your life raft. It's not necessarily about the act itself; it's about what me-time gives you afterwards.

Having me-time helps you stay calm when one of the kids spills their bowl of spaghetti on the floor or has a diaper blow-out just as you're walking out the door.

Personally, I think every mom deserves to have at *least* fifteen to thirty minutes of decompressed me-time **every single day**.

On top of that, I think an extended hour-long me-time appointment to get out and do something at least once a week would be a great self-care recipe.

In a perfect world, I think we should actually have

an hour every day...but something is better than nothing right? At least that's what I keep telling myself anyway.

In order to truly enjoy your me-time you have to be honest about what things make you feel recharged and good about yourself. Likewise, it's important you ask yourself what drains your energy too.

In all honesty, you will never "have time" for me-time. So you can't wait until all of your work is "done", otherwise you'll never get to go play.

Initially, building me-time into your routine isn't always easy and can be quite the challenge. Try to remind yourself of the reward though. Watch how good you feel when you come back from me-time. Eventually you'll get more comfortable with it.

Putting Me-Time In Your Calendar

When it comes to hair appointments, for the most part we wouldn't think about rescheduling or cancelling those. Probably because there's nothing quite like walking into the salon with a ratted pony tail and walking out with hair that's actually *done*. Come to think of it, I usually time my hair appointments so that I can go pick my son up from school right afterwards. But what I think I'll do from this day forward is time it so that I'm meeting my husband for a date night, or another mom friend out for a coffee or happy-hour drink. I mean, why waste hair that got all done up by someone else. I don't know why I didn't think of that before!

Ok, sorry.

Getting back on track---

My point is...there's a long list of appointments we would never think to cancel or reschedule.

Like our kids doctors' appointments, their haircuts, playdates, and even our car maintenance appointments.

But why do we --- hardworking busy moms have such a hard time believing that "me-time" is even *more* important than all the things above?

The reason is this: we don't see "me time" as a valuable time investment.

We look at it as less important.

If you haven't put a "me-time" appointment in your calendar in the last three to six months but you've faithfully taken your car into the shop to get an oil change...then you hold your car at a higher priority than yourself.

You might be viewing "me-time" as a luxury, but it's not. It's a necessity.

In the throes of parenting and building my business, it seemed nearly impossible to squeeze in "me time". This is why most of the time I avoided it.

But eventually I was forced to look at where, who, and what I was spending my time on.

In a nutshell, I spent my time on everybody else but myself.

I started to see that "me time" wasn't going to squeeze itself into my calendar.

I knew I had to make "me time" an important priority.

Once it got into my calendar, I was committed to keeping it there the same way I would if I had to take one of the kids to the doctor.

The more I practiced this, the calmer, cool, and collected I felt.

Essentially, I was rebooting my computer and recharging my mom batteries.

I found I was less reactive to the nuisances of parenting and in my business.

I was more peaceful and I began to feel whole again.

I became more loving and patient with my family and friends.

And, I felt way less resentful.

The other evening around 8 pm, my twelve-year-old son came into my bedroom.

From 8 pm – 9 pm is the household quiet time. He can read, draw, stare at the walls.... I don't really care, but 9 PM is when he's expected to turn the lights out and go to sleep.

I was in the midst of my own "me time" when he made his way to me.

He came into our room, plopped himself on our bed and started chatting (which is something I actually adore).

But, I was right in the middle of writing, which was my form of "me time" in that moment.

I stopped what I was doing, gave him my undivided attention, replied and then politely said "OK, I'm having some 'me time' right now so can we pick this conversation up in the morning?"

His reply?

"But Mommmmm..."

And he continued talking.

"I understand, but you know how sometimes you just like to do your own thing sometimes?"

"Yeah?"

"When you do that, I don't take it personal because I know that doesn't take away from the love you have for me, it's just that you need some time to yourself. Right?"

"Yeah."

"Well, Mom likes to do her own thing sometimes too. And that will never, ever take away from the love I have for you. Actually, it'll only make it grow more."

He stood up, began to exit and said *"OK. Goodnight. Love you."*

I didn't feel bad about any of this either.

Kids aren't aware that their parents need time to themselves.

Through their eyes we're there to serve them day and night. Let's face it though, that's because we've programmed them this way.

I want my boys to grow up knowing the importance of having their own "me time"; whether they're three years old, twelve, twenty, or ninety.

I don't want them to get all caught up in the demands of life and lose sight of themselves.

For me, this means I have to be willing to speak up for myself and to teach through example that "me time" is in fact an important part of a healthy life.

Actually, I take that back.

It's not "important".

It's *vital*.

Me-time doesn't take away from anything or anyone; it's an investment of time into you.

Take a look at your upcoming week and carve out one hour this week for self-care, whatever that means for you.

If one hour seems like too much, start with 15 minutes.

Just be sure to add **something** for "me time".

Put it in your calendar.

Me-time happens in increments, so don't make this complicated.

Take me for example…writing is a form of my me-time. This book you're reading right now was written in **many** *increments*. If I sat down and thought I had to write this book all in one sitting or that it would be done by tomorrow, you wouldn't be reading it. It never would've happened.

Instead, I had to sprinkle those writing (me-time) moments here and there throughout my days.

My point is, those small moments to yourself *add*

up. They make much more of an impact than you might think.

Remember, the time you carve out for yourself is about YOU.

Not about the things on your to-do list. Treat this time as you would your kids' dentist appointment or an important meeting.

You wouldn't think of cancelling or rescheduling those so easily, right?

What If I Feel Like I've Lost Myself to My Kids?

I once had a coaching client whom I'll call "Sally".

She went to college, traveled around Europe for a while, and then got married in her mid-twenties.

The natural progression for her was to start a family.

And with good intentions, Sally devoted nearly all of her love, time, and energy into making her family happy.

She and her husband went from being "Sally and Mike" to "Mom and Dad" in the blink of an eye.

Their lives became so intertwined that after a few years, there was little distinction between who Sally was and who her husband was. They slowly began to melt into one and at the same time, drift away from each other.

They were married for nearly twenty years when their youngest went off to college.

Sally told me she felt as if she had lost a limb.

She had no idea what to do with herself. She felt lost, as if a piece of her died as she got her son settled into his new dorm room.

For months, she felt heartbroken.

"Who am I?" She repeatedly asked herself over and over.

She once told me during a coaching session *"I spent so much time taking care of everybody else, I don't even **how** to take care of myself anymore."*

But – we worked together and she slowly picked away at the art of self-care and began to redefine who she was.

It didn't take her long to start feeling reconnected. She began getting excited about this next chapter of her life. She felt for the first time in a long time that this was HER time.

She felt lighter and resumed old creative projects she once loved to do before she ever had kids.

Like painting, gardening, and fixing up old furniture.

Sally's story is like so many women who get married and have kids.

There seems to be this preconceived notion that having kids means doing things for everybody else and pushing yourself off to the side until the kids leave the house.

Kids, no kids, furry four-legged kids or no furry four-legged kids - your inner light must continue to be fed.

The gift that Sally's kids left her as they set out on their own life adventures was the ability to reconnect with the truth of who **she** was.

The key to all healthy relationships is this: love yourself first, then others.

Where Do I Start?

Right where you are.

Before we get into developing a self-care practice, it's important to first shed some light on the things that will keep you from "self-caring".

If you don't know the blocks that will keep you away from tending to yourself, it makes it exceptionally hard to create a self-care practice that will become a part of your daily routine.

So for now, hang tight and just keep reading.

We'll get to the self-care action plan in a jiffy.

Intellectually, you might be saying *"Yeah I know I need self-care."* but are you acting on it?

There are so many barriers that can come between you and your self-care practice. If you crave more peace, joy, and overall happiness, then let's take a look at these three blocks that could be derailing your self-care routine.

1 – "Self-care is Selfish."

If you took one-hundred dollars from your family savings account and gave it to me to invest and then I turned around a year later and gave you back five-hundred dollars, would that be selfish of you? Of course not. Why? Because there's value in it.

Self-care is a bit trickier to see the value because you can't touch it or hold it like you can dollars. But the value of it is not diminished just because you can't "see" the value.

Self-care does not take away from anyone or anything. It adds value to; you, your family, and to the world around you.

It's really that simple.

It's not a matter of *"I either take care of you or I take care of me."* It's more like *"If I don't take care of me, I don't have anything left to take care of you with."* The point I'm going to keep driving home in this book is that self-care is an investment, of time. You have to truly believe that in order to take action.

2 – "It Takes too Much Time."

As moms, we tend to overcomplicate things. We make little things into big things and it's no different when it comes to our self-care routine.

The truth is, self-care does take time out of your day.

But you get to choose how much time you want, or have to spend on it. It doesn't matter if its 5 minutes or 50 minutes, work with what you've got and do what feels comfortable. The amount of time isn't as important as it is that you're doing *something* for yourself.

Every time you find yourself saying *"there's not enough time"*, I want you to replace it with *"that's not a priority for me."*

This will shine the light on where your priorities are, and have been. The truth of the matter is, there's *plenty* of time in your busy day to tend to yourself, but it hasn't been a big priority for you.

It's that everyone and everything else has likely been *more* of a priority.

You can find 30 seconds to take a few big deep breaths. You can sneak in five minutes to soak up some sunshine or listen to your favorite meditation, music, or inspirational podcast.

You have time for self-care.

You just have to believe there's time.

Affirm *"I have plenty of time to self-care."*

3 – "I Don't Know What to Do."

Maybe that's true. You're not sure what to do because you spend most of your days taking care of everyone else around you.

Start by giving yourself just 5 minutes in the morning and ask yourself *"What do I need to feel good today?"* *"How can I care, love, and nurture myself today?"*

Listen to and honor the answers that come up.

Here are some ideas to get you started: a walk in nature, a meditation, quiet prayer, a bubble bath with essential oils, journaling, enjoying a slice of your favorite cheesecake from the upscale place down the street.

You know what you need, just give yourself permission to go after it.

I also created a list of 101 Ways to Self-Care that you can download.

Check it out: amommyreboot.com

What About The Guilt I Feel?

"Mom guilt" is the mother of all guilt (pun intended) and can be one of the biggest barriers to your self-care practice.

Like the many other emotions and feelings we feel, it only exists in the mind though. Guilt isn't tangible. You can't touch it nor hold it. And if I asked you to bring me a cup of it, you certainly couldn't.

Although guilt feels as real as the cup you hold in your hand, it's a mere thought.

As kick ass as we are, we really "shouldn't" feel guilty about ANYTHING.

But we do!

It's a mom thing and we feel guilty about *everything*.

As soon as we become a mom, our sentences suddenly start with *"I feel bad that…"*

- My kid doesn't feel good

- I picked him up late from daycare

- I grounded him

- He had cereal for dinner

- She's sad

- He's so upset

- I put her to bed early

- She didn't get picked for the team

- I let her watch a ton of Netflix

- I let him play too many video games

- I didn't make him eat his vegetables

- Blah

- Blah

- Blah

The guilt, the feeling bad, the wondering if we're doing a good job - it's non-stop.

Most of it's not even spoken out loud either; we just keep it stored in our pretty little heads.

Especially when it comes to trying to do anything for ourselves, that tends to bring up a whole other level of mom-guilt. It's as if we take the guilt fairy with us to meet a girlfriend and we put her on our shoulder. As we sit across from our friend sipping a glass of wine pretending to listen, it chatters. *"I wonder if the baby's sleeping yet? I'm not going to be there to read his bed-time story. Maybe I should head home earlier. I bet he's in the bath right now. He's probably crying for me. I should text {insert baby-sitter or partner's name here} to check on the kids..."*

Instead of really enjoying the breather, we consume our thoughts with guilt. We focus our energy on what we're *not* doing instead of what we <u>are</u> doing; which is taking a well-deserved break.

For years I struggled with guilt anytime I did something for myself. I felt the time to myself was taking *away* from my family.

Mom guilt is inevitable.

Like swollen breasts and leaky boobs are a part of pregnancy and post-partum, guilt is also a part of your mom journey.

You don't get mad at your uncooperative boobs; you just accept them for what they are and deal with them. You don't let them ruin your life. It's more like *"Oh hey look, my boobs are leaking."*

Mom guilt is just something we'll always have to deal with.

That doesn't mean we need to let it run our lives though. We can acknowledge it and then choose to kick guilt out of the driver's seat.

So let's peel back the layers of mom-guilt.

One of the reasons mom guilt prevents you from going to a yoga class, meeting a friend for lunch, or hiring a sitter so you can sit in your bedroom and watch your favorite show in peace and quiet is because you think on some level you're being *selfish*.

Feeling selfish is at the core of mom guilt.

I used to believe that the more I did for everybody else, the more I sacrificed – *the better mom I was.*

Again, I had it all backwards. I know now that's total B.S and antiquated thinking.

I've learned what in fact makes me a good mom is being kind, loving, and patient towards my kids.

To be mindful and have the patience to sit and really listen to what they have to say rather than only half listen because I'm burnt out and exhausted – *that's* what makes me a good mom and *that's* what they will remember.

It's not in the *doing*. It's not the things I get done or cross off my to-do list, it's how I show up to my kids.

It's how I am *being*. That's what's <u>most</u> important and what will impact them.

What makes me a good mom is having the energy to handle the "hideousness" of life and all its struggles.

Being a good mom means to be less reactive to the chaos around me. I can't do that if I don't give myself mini-breaks to breathe every once in a while though.

What makes me a good mom is being a positive example for my kids.

I have to be at the helm and let my kids see me doing things I love and that fill up my cup. One day they'll have families of their own and I don't want my boys to lose sight of their passions and the importance of taking care of themselves. Not now, not ever.

Sure, I could sit down and tell them all the great things I know about self-care, but what good would that do. Like most of my lectures longer than five minutes, they'll just tune me out.

All they'll hear is "Blah, blah, blah…"

So instead, I lead by example. Our kids notice a lot more than we give them credit for. My kids see the mom who retreats into her bedroom for a few minutes after a long day versus the mom who comes out. *Being* the example is much more powerful than carrying on and on trying to explain the importance of self-care.

I'm a better mom and a better person when I give myself permission to self-care. It's the things like moving my body, taking walks alone on the beach, writing, meditating, chatting or spending time with my girlfriends and having date nights with my husband that make me feel good.

Sure, I want my kids to have clean clothes and eat healthy meals, but at the end of the day all I really want is for my kids to feel L.O.V.E.

How can I truly give that to them unless I have it within myself first?

So knowing all of this, why in the world is there any reason to feel guilty about the time I take to self-care?

The other night I was getting ready in my bathroom; I was enjoying my own little private retreat. I had just finished a long day of coaching calls, writing, and meeting deadlines for my freelance clients.

We decided to go to a baseball game --- on a school night. I know! Crazy right?

I don't know about you, but I LOVE getting ready - by myself. I really get into it. It's become this fun form of self-care for me.

I listen to music, I try on different outfits, I slap some makeup on, I remove the pony tail I've been wearing since yesterday, and I prettify myself.

It's fun.

Plus, we needed to leave soon, so I was trying to hurry up too.

Well, in came my twelve-year son asking me a ton of questions about all the things he could have asked me during the thirty-minute drive commute on our way home from school less than an hour ago.

I love chatting with my kids, but his timing was way off.

First of all, he just threw my door open (without knocking) and started chatting away.

After I reminded him to knock, I didn't think too much of it at first. I instantaneously started answering his questions and chit chatting back with him.

But then I noticed I just wanted him to stop talking.

I started to get so annoyed that he was in my space and interrupting me. I wasn't even really listening to him. I was too busy judging and ranting in my own head.

For me, that's a red flag.

Deep down, I knew it really wasn't about him. It was about me and what was going on inside.

I realized I wasn't setting boundaries and I was becoming resentful about it.

I began feeling annoyed because I was <u>dishonoring</u> myself.

That wasn't really his fault, it was mine.

So I stopped him mid-sentence.

"Hey bud, is there any way you could please give me like fifteen minutes? I really need to finish getting ready, I've had a long day, and I just need a little bit of alone time right now."

He said *"Noooo, but I want to hang out in here with you."*

{Queue the mom guilt.}

"I know you do. And I want to hang out with you too. But right now I just need you to step out and I'll come back out as soon as I'm done. I just need fifteen more minutes. Ok?" As I'm saying this, I gently took his hand and began to guide him out my bedroom door because he wasn't taking no for an answer.

He finally realized I was serious, *"Ok fineeeeee...."*

And then just before I shut the door behind him, I said *"I love you. Thank you."*

Now the door was closed <u>and</u> locked.

For a millisecond I felt bad. I quickly reminded myself that I really needed this brief moment alone to decompress.

And then it was gone.

POOF!

There was no reason for me to start judging myself or feel any sort of shame around this.

I let it go.

I knew I had to put myself first and I was the only one who could do that.

I returned to my music and finished getting ready. I felt really good about honoring my needs and standing up for them. When I returned to the living room fifteen minutes later, I felt refreshed and ready to go. I was eager to have those conversations with him.

I was mindful and so much more present - which is ultimately what he _needed_ from me at the time.

So, not only was it a gift to me, it was a gift to *him* too.

I started taking these mini bedroom retreats when he was about five years old. So for the most part he's used to them.

A few months ago, after having just coming out of another mini bedroom retreat and kicking him out again, I asked him *"Do you think I'm a bad mom or are your feelings hurt when I kick you out of my room to take a few deep breaths?"* He replied, *"Nooooo, why would I think that?"* (His tone was as if I asked him if I had a purple head.)

I got **that** kind of NO.

He added, "Well, sometimes my feelings get hurt, but only for a second and then it goes away because sometimes I need to be alone too."

Our kids really don't care as much as we think they do. It's us creating these big ugly stories in our own heads.

It's not like my kid is going to look back and say, *"Oh my God, I remember this one time my mom was getting ready and she asked me to give her fifteen minutes because she needed her space. Now I need therapy."*

That just won't happen. It's crazy to think about all the scenarios we create inside our beautiful mom minds.

Taking care of you does not take away from anyone, or anything. It adds **value**.

Remember, taking care of <u>you</u> IS taking care of the kids.

If we truly know that … not just intellectually but at the core of our being, then there's no reason to feel guilty.

<u>Now What??</u>

1.) Acknowledge the guilt - don't try to resist it. The more you try to shove down these feelings, the more they'll surface. It's OK if you feel the way you do. Guilt is a human emotion. Just say *"I see your guilt"* and don't dwell on it. Once you acknowledge the emotion, you can decide to kick it out of the driver's seat. Remember, guilt is just a thought you can control.

2.) Behind every guilty feeling is a fear. So an empowering question you could ask yourself is *"What fear is behind the way that I'm feeling right now?"* Shedding light on our fears often dissolves them. You might be fearing what other people will think, how someone might react, or disappointing someone. At the end of the day though, you have to live your life authentically. The reality is, you *will* disappoint along the way. It's just a part of self-care. Get comfy with it.

3.) This mantra will help to dissolve guilt: *"I will honor myself by taking care of my own needs every day. This will make me happier and more able to care of my family. I will be a good example to my kids so they know when we are kind to ourselves, we can easily be kind to others."* Put it on your bathroom mirror.

How Do I Honor My Own Needs?

It was March and I started to think about how I wanted to spend my upcoming Mother's Day. I thought about taking the kids to go see my mom two hours away, but that wasn't it. I thought about having my husband's family over for a brunch, but that felt like too much work. I thought about asking my husband to make reservations at a fancy restaurant so neither one of us had to cook, but an overcrowded restaurant didn't seem fun either.

Finally, it hit me. When I got **brutally** honest with myself....I didn't want to spend the whole time with my kids and I didn't want "stuff" either. I have plenty of candles, lotions, and nail polish already. Pretty flowers and cards my husband picks out from my kids all sounds good on paper and it even looks great on social media.

However, once I worked through all the judgements I had about myself I realized I wanted nothing more than to spend a night at the beach. At first I thought I'd go by myself. Then I realized I'd love to spend it with my own mom. I wanted a day off! No kids, no responsibilities and nobody to answer to. Just us, the beach, a hotel pool, and no agenda. I see my mom throughout the year, but I always have the kids with me. So it's rare we get to complete an uninterrupted conversation together. I hardly ever feel like I get to spend good quality time with her when everyone's around.

Oh, and I also wanted to come home to a clean house too. {Go big or go home right?}

We met bright and early on Saturday morning and came home mid-day on Sunday, which was Mother's Day. So I had plenty of time to spend time with my family.

Once I OWNED what I craved so badly, I was able to let go of any guilt and I told my husband exactly what I wanted. I didn't feel ashamed or wishy-washy either. I knew damn well that I deserved it; as did my mom. I booked the hotel and we were literally counting down the days. It was so nice just having the trip to look forward to.

We had the **best** time. Both of us are planners by nature, but neither one of us wanted to plan anything. So we didn't. We just winged it. We hung by the pool, we day drank, we laughed, we had uninterrupted chats, we walked on the beach, we enjoyed lovely meals and then later we lounged in the room and watched our favorite shows. We even caught an early matinee movie and had lunch before parting ways.

When I came home from our 36 hour beach trip....I felt SO REFRESHED and I had a new appreciation for my beautiful children and hubby.

{If my story is something that appeals to you, I *highly* suggest doing it.) If you don't really like your mom, go with a mom friend or a group of mom friends. If you want to be by yourself, go by yourself. If you can't afford a hotel, save or work with what you've got. Have a staycation and lock yourself in a spare room or plan a sleepover at a friend's house and send the kids somewhere else. Plan a day out with other mom friends. If you want to spend the day antiquing then go antiquing. If you want to go for a drive, go drive around by yourself and jam your favorite music. If you need to hire a babysitter for the day because you're husband isn't on board, then do that too. If you're worried *"what other family members might think"* --- screw them. This is YOUR Mother's Day, not theirs. Let them judge if they want. Holidays are the worst when it comes to doing things we don't really want to do in order to serve our family; both immediate and extended. Wanting and craving a day off doesn't make you a bad mom so let that go now. This is the ONE day a year that is YOURS, so why spend it doing anything other than what *YOU* <u>want</u> to do! It's never too early to decide what you want for next year. (Especially if last Mother's Day sucked.) Be brave, go after what your heart desires and don't let that inner critic stand in your way. You've got this!}

Listen and honor yourself; your mind, body and spirit.

In order to tell others what you need, first you yourself have to know what **you** want.

You have to be in touch with who you are and what it takes for you to be happy. Staying true to you is where you'll find the most happiness. The things you like, the things you don't like, and paying attention to the things that push you over the edge are indicators on your happiness trail.

If you don't know what you need, how will you ever be able to express how you feel to others?

The other day one of our dogs had to go to the vet. The hubby was awesome and offered to take her.

When he returned from the vet though, he explained what was wrong with her (an ear infection) and told me that she needed to take an antibiotic three times a day for fourteen days.

Then, he ever so gently squeezed in these words *"Could you put a reminder in your phone for me to give it to her three times a day. Maybe 8am, 1pm, and 6pm?"*

He was dead serious.

And instinctively, I almost actually did it too.

Then I thought *"Wait a second! What would be the point of that? That's the last thing I needed, something **else** to micromanage. Maybe he's joking?"*

He wasn't.

"Seriously?" I asked.

"Yeah, it's really important that she gets it at the same time each day."

He was still super serious.

"Sooooo, what's wrong with your phone?"

"I might forget," he replied.

*"Not if you put a reminder in <u>your</u> calendar you won't. Nice try buddy. Sooooo - I need **you** to put a reminder in **your** calendar to give her the medicine. Please. And thanks."*

I was dead serious while he was half-smirking now.

Could I have easily taken on that task?

You betcha'.

But why?

Why would I do that to myself?

My week was already packed with tons of my own stuff already. Just like his.

My to-do list could not take one more thing to be added.

I knew that.

I also knew that we've had this long-standing agreement...

While we both pitch in to help the other, my primary job beyond my business, is the majority of anything to do with the kids. Such as doctor appointments, haircuts, trips to the dentist, school stuff...

Beyond his business stuff and various household items, are the *dogs*.

I delegated that a few years ago and it has worked beautifully ever since.

He clearly forgot about that so it was my job to remind him.

So when he politely asked me to *"add this to my calendar"* I had two choices:

1. Do it and take the risk of being overwhelmed and somewhat resentful about it later.

2. Be willing to speak my needs and stand up for them. Despite what he might think or how his life might be "inconvenienced".

If this was ten, or even just five years ago - I would have mindlessly opted for number one.

But, I know this doesn't serve <u>anybody</u>, especially

our marriage.

It's not always easy to say NO though.

Sure, sometimes I feel like the "bad guy".

I learned to be OK with that because it's usually short-lived.

What's most important in the long-term is my ability to honor my needs and speak my truth (in the most loving and gentle way possible, of course).

Nobody but me knows what I need in any given moment.

I'm the one who has to be willing to say no.

It's not a selfish act, it an act of self-care and self-love.

When I take care of myself I can better take care of others and offer even *more* love to those around me.

Just the other day, while I was right smack dab in the middle of cleaning the house my twelve-year old son asked if he could have a sandwich.

"Sure, go help yourself. There's plenty in the fridge to pick from." I prompted him.

"But I want you to make it for me." He quickly replied.

"I'm in the middle of something right now bud; you'll need to make it yourself."

"I don't feel like it though." While he hangs on the refrigerator door he moans *"Never mind. I just won't eat then."*

This would've bothered me before. I definitely would've stopped what I was doing so I could make it for him. I mean *"What kind of mom would I be to let him go hungry?"*

The reality is though, he's not going to starve himself to death; he'll eventually eat when he's hungry. He won't die from a skipped Saturday lunch any more than this means I'm a bad mom because I didn't make it for him.

Ultimately this is his problem, not mine.

I know, that might sound harsh.

This isn't even really about the sandwich or even me being in the middle of something though. This is about me knowing my needs and ultimately wanting my kids to be self-reliant and self-sufficient.

If I continue to do *everything* for them when they're perfectly capable, I'm not helping them -- I'm hindering them.

In the name of love, we feel this constant pull to do everything for our kids. When in reality, it slows their growth and progress.

I joke around with both my boys and say, *"Your wives are going to thank me one day."*

Seriously though, you have to be in tune and ask yourself *"**What do I need right now?**"*

If the answer coming up is *"help"* then be willing to ask for it.

If the answer is *to "laugh"*, then go call a girlfriend or watch a funny movie.

If the answer that comes up is, *"sleep"* then give yourself permission to rest for 15 minutes.

You really don't need to get <u>everything</u> done today.

Sure, you'll always have things on your list that you absolutely need to get done. But most of the time, we just keep adding endless tasks because we think we're some kind of super hero.

So do the things that need to get done, and then give yourself what you need.

I call myself a recovering type A perfectionist. In the beginning of my self-care journey, I struggled with not having everything crossed off for the day.

I still have some of those tendencies, but being aware of them allows me to keep them from controlling my life.

The side of me who feels like happiness is getting it all done "perfectly", and marking things off my to-do list, is a total unrealistic control freak. I know that now.

I also know that above all else my *self-care* is the most important thing of all.

I know once I intentionally do things to take care of myself, I'll have the mental clarity, capacity, and energy to deal with everything that's hitting me in the face.

Be aware and willing to say to yourself every once in a while, *"It's OK that I'm not going to get everything done. It will never be all done."*

Honor the voice within and learn to let go.

Now What??

1.) Keep this question at the forefront of your mind today…*"What do I need right now?"* Be willing to honor the answers that come up. Know the things that will keep you from honoring them are your fears and a mind that sees the impossibilities rather than the possibilities.

2.) Go after what you need and know that by doing so, you are serving your family as well.

How Do I Live By a Standard of Grace Rather than Perfection?

Sometimes I just have to get out of my own head and go for a walk.

Even if it feels like it's 1,000 degrees outside. (I live in Florida)

Even if it feels like I've made no progress on my to-do list or pursued any of my big dreams! I.e. writing this book.

Sometimes, it's more about <u>being</u> than it is *doing*.

Sometimes being gentle and kind to myself becomes the single most important thing I do all day.

Being graceful is a state of mind, not a state of physical perfection.

In order to cultivate a graceful heart you have to be good to yourself, and simply accept yourself.

In a world of social media and chasing visions of a perfect life, that can feel so unattainable. On one hand we see others seemingly living a life of their dreams so we feel like we can have it too, but then on the other, it's easy to feel bad that "we aren't there yet."

Two days after my fortieth birthday this past year, I was in my gynecologist's office scheduling a hysterectomy.

Oh, the irony of that.

I knew it was coming. We had taken several other paths over the years to try to avoid it but it was time, and I was ready.

The surgery would require a night stay in the hospital and a recovery time of 6-8 weeks.

Mentally, I prepared myself. But I don't think my family did.

I tried to warn them.

There was a slew of activities I wouldn't be able to do post-op.

Like drive. My youngest son's school was a thirty-minute commute each way. My hubs usually did the morning and I did the afternoons to help split it up. But for two weeks, driving was off limits for me.

For a full six to eight weeks, I wasn't allowed to push or pull; which meant neither vacuuming nor mopping. As far as picking up things, "nothing heavier than a gallon of milk". So, no baskets full of laundry, my dog, nor groceries from the car.

I thought ahead and did what any good mom would do though...I called in my own mom for some help.

My mom stayed with us for about five days. She handled all the meals and helped my hubby around the house too. The amount of quality time we spent together was something I'll always cherish. We spent a lot of time chatting, and snuggling on the couch binge watching movies and TV shows.

The only physical activity I was allowed to do as much as I could tolerate, was walking.

Lucky for me, that's one of my favorite activities to do. When I wasn't resting, I was walking.

My physical recovery went exceptionally well. I walked over a mile to lunch with my mom not even forty-eight hours after surgery.

I was utterly amazed at how great I felt and how quickly my body healed.

My only real complaint was how tired I felt. I was exhausted!

I suppose that was because my body was working overtime to heal itself.

A couple days after my mom left (about one-week post-op), I was up making my lunch and my husband asked, *"Do you want to help me pick up the house a bit?"*

I rolled his words around in my head for a second and really thought about his request.

"Nope. Not feeling up to it right now."

And I had no problems telling him so.

Now, to *say* that was one thing.

To say that with zero guilt took years of practice and countless failures.

Even though I felt great, I knew there was a fine line of pushing myself too hard. And that was the last thing I wanted to do.

I knew my long-term recovery was solely dependent on the actions I took in the early days.

Even if I felt good, I knew I had to take it easy.

On one hand I couldn't believe my husband had the gonads to ask me to help clean up the house. On the other hand, I couldn't really blame him either. I mean, he saw me up and about and figured I was fine to help.

I was sending him mixed messages so I knew it was up to me to set the record straight.

Could have I helped and pushed through it?

Probably.

But for what?

The sake of his feelings?

I knew I was the one responsible for taking care of myself. I couldn't leave it up to my husband to tell me how much was too much.

I have no doubt in my mind that if it were up to him, I would've been back on my feet and in the full swing of things by now.

But I knew I wasn't ready and I just had to accept that.

My recovery was hard; on me, on my husband, and on our marriage.

Slowing down in life isn't a bad thing. As you'll learn more throughout this book, slowing down is something I had a real problem with.

Somewhere along the way, I decided I could have it all and I would do it all perfectly. I had this "perfect" image in my mind to raise my kids perfectly, have the perfect marriage, and simultaneously chase my "perfect dreams". This chasing perfection thing is what led me to almost burning out though. I felt exhausted, and empty inside.

It wasn't until I learned that by slowing down, I can make intentional decisions to simplify by choosing what matters the most.

Living by a standard of grace rather than perfection allows me to acknowledge that I'm human and I have human flaws. It means for me, that I aim to maintain the truth of who I am both personally and professionally. If this means others don't like me or disagree with me, then so be it.

I'm not perfect and I get better and better at forgiving myself for that.

Living gracefully and releasing perfection means that I'm relentless about making decisions that brings peace to my soul so I can feel free.

I love everything to be in its place, I'm that girl who's always trying to pick up the house. So this means that I sometimes leave the housework for another time. I do it because the more I practice the art of grace not perfection, the more I realize that true joy isn't in having everything tidy, it's in enjoying the present moment.

I don't have to be perfect to embrace the gifts of grace. Grace is for the flawed and the undeserving.

In the days of my healing, I kept grace at the top of my priority list. Especially when I knew I was leaning on my husband to do more and pick up my slack.

Instead of feeling bad about it, it was just a matter of resting when I got tired, allowing myself to enjoy a good book at a time I would normally be doing other things, saying NO, asking for help more often, and being OK with the fact that I wasn't at the top of my game.

Now What??

1.) Know that perfectionism is a myth and it robs you of your joyful moments. Be ok that you don't "have it together" all the time. You are flawed and so am I. But we're awesome anyway!

2.) Carry this affirmation with you or tape it on your bathroom mirror or car visor: ***"I will hold myself to a standard of grace, not perfection."***

How do I Get More Comfortable with Asking for Help?

I think when it comes to parenting; a partnership is what most women crave.

It doesn't matter if it's with their husband, their boyfriend, or even an ex. Most women just want to feel that they're not alone in this parenting thing.

I've coached so many moms who've held onto a ton of resentment towards their husbands and significant others.

Their chief complaint…*"I don't get enough help."*

One of my jobs as a good coach is to ask bold questions that will stretch my clients. When I dare ask *"What have you done to contribute to this?"* it's then I usually hear a long list of reasons such as…

"Well, my husband is the breadwinner and he works really hard. <u>My</u> job is to take care of the kids."

Or, *"He's hardly ever home because he's working so much. I have no choice but to do as much as I do."*

Even though there's circumstantial truth to these

answers, we have to be willing to dig deeper.

Radical self-care requires women to stand up and say *"I can't be the best I can be if I don't have time for myself."*

It boils down to just three small, but oh so powerful words.

I NEED HELP!

Why is asking for help so damn hard for us moms.

We plan vacations, we read stories and tuck our kids in at night, we research sicknesses, we send out birthday cards, and plan birthday parties. We think about holiday gifts and figure out who's going to get what. We shop. We sign school papers, we show up to volunteer, we attend school conferences, we micromanage and help with homework, we clean the house, we take kids to the dentist and the doctor.

We take our kids to play-dates and friends' houses. We cart them back and forth from sports and other extracurricular activities. We make sure they're brushing their teeth, bathe and shower. We kiss boo-boos. We pay the bills, grocery shop, and run businesses. We work full-time, we handle school drop offs and pick-ups. We figure out what's for dinner, wipe snotty noses and we deal with tears and tantrums.

Yet we still don't feel like we need or deserve

help?

The things I listed are but a *fraction* of the physical stuff we do; I didn't even mention the endless *emotional* support we give our kids and family.

Now, this isn't to say our husbands and partners don't help us out. At least I'm hoping that's *not* the case. My point is, everything mostly feels like it's on us. Even if it's not true, we feel like it is.

Our lists are endless.

This is why we can't blame our partners nor expect them to be mind-readers.

We are the ones responsible for our own well-being.

Nobody but you knows how you're feeling.

Nobody but you're knows when you're on the verge of burnout or tears.

Nobody but you knows the running list of tasks continuously firing off in your head.

Nobody but you knows when it's time for a break.

Asking for and accepting help is <u>not</u> a weakness.

It takes a great amount of strength and courage to

ask for and receive help.

Now What??

1.) Know your limits.

2.) Ask for help.

3.) Graciously accept help.

How Do I Set Boundaries?

Without my lists, I'd flounder and forget to do the important things.

If I'm being honest though, I always have things on my list that aren't as important as I think they are.

For instance, there are times that sleep comes before laundry but only laundry makes it on the list.

Learning to give ourselves permission to focus on what's <u>really</u> important is essential to self-care.

And what's **most** important, is *YOU*.

If you eliminate the unessential responsibilities off your (written or internal) list, this will not only create some extra time and space, it will also help lift the burden of the feeling that you're failing to keep up with everything.

I can't tell you the number of times that I had my day fully mapped out on my pretty little list.

On paper, it all appeared to be very important.

Then, life happened.

Other things became more of a priority and I went to bed beating myself up that *"everything didn't get done."*

Looking back at my day though, I went on a morning run around the lake, I wrote a good portion of my book, I had a coaching call with a client, and after I picked my son up early from school because he didn't feel good I laid with him on the couch.

Sure, maybe I didn't run to the post office or vacuum out the car like I had on my list, but were those things *really* more important than what I *did* get accomplished?

Heck no!

Feeling overwhelmed can quickly send us spiraling downwards into self-loathing hell.

When you decide to put yourself first, you have to be willing to say no to the unimportant things in your life so you can say YES to yourself.

With so many modern life demands, it's really easy to push yourself off.

It usually isn't until we get sick or we become so overwhelmed with life that the only thing we have the energy to do is binge watch our favorite shows or thumb through social media.

It's then we might finally realize we haven't been giving ourselves the same love and attention we've been so easily giving everybody else.

Taking care of ourselves isn't selfish - it's *practical*.

For moms around the world, there's this underlying pull that we could, or *"should"* be doing things for someone else more than ourselves.

When this feeling of "should" pops up, remind yourself of this: *"Taking care of myself allows me to better care for my kids and family."*

I have these words taped to my bathroom mirror and other random places to help remind me of this.

Sometimes you might start thinking that self-care means you have to plan these mammoth time-consuming tasks.

But in truth, the best action steps towards taking good care of you are through small meaningful, baby steps.

Daily.

Things like sitting for five minutes to write down three things you're grateful for or taking a few minutes before you wake up the kids to take a couple deep breaths and set your intentions for the day.

Whatever you decide, catering to yourself in small increments like this will pay off big time for you and those around you.

I was on the phone with my mom one day.

Knowing both my husband and I work from

home, she asked what we do for lunch.

"Do you make his lunch for him?"

"If I have time and if I feel like it." I replied.

She laughed.

I began explaining that if I took on the role of "lunch maker", he would get accustomed to that and expect his lunch to be made every-day.

And I just can't do that.

I'm not a stay-at-home mom; I'm a mom who works from home and I have to protect my work time.

Sure, he's {currently} the "bread-winner" and I might be the "main parent", but I take my writing, coaching and building my business very seriously.

If I didn't, who else would?

We're both busy, and we are both caregivers.

I shared this story with my mom …

Just the other day I had blocked time out in my schedule to sit down and write this book.

I knew I only had a small window of time before I had to pick up my son from school.

Knowing this week was going to be a busy one, I made a boat load of chicken for the week so I could have quick easy meals for busy days ahead.

I was in the kitchen making my lunch (which is right next to his office area), and my husband peeked his head around the corner, and asked *"Are you making lunch?"*

"Yep. But you're going to have to make your own today babe. I need to sit down to write in a few minutes so I'm just grabbing something really quick."

He jokingly looked down at our wiener dog, who was patiently waiting for some food to drop and said *"Sorry Peanut, that lunch is only for Mommy."*

He said it "jokingly" but we all know he was at least *half* serious.

I didn't take any offense to it though, because it was the truth.

In that moment I was being selfish enough to honor the pursuit of my big goals.

This book isn't going to write itself.

I know that if I'm not protective of my writing times or willing to draw boundaries, then the calling to write this book will never be fulfilled.

In essence, I would be dishonoring myself and that's the last thing I want.

Being a mom who's committed to caring for

herself, means you must be *disciplined*. You have to *own* your shit.

I know for a fact that I very easily could have made my husband's lunch that day.

This wasn't about lunch though; it was about something much bigger.

It's about doing things that give me life, and *writing* is one of them.

If I let my husband's (or kids) needs *constantly* get in the way of my own, you wouldn't be reading this book right now.

And *you*, the reader of this book is really important to me.

Being a writer, allowing creativity to flow through me, expressing my truths, sharing my wisdom, and helping others, is what I'm wired for.

I know I have to stay true to that and I'm the one responsible for it; nobody else.

My mom replied, *"Oh my God, I could never do that."*

I don't really believe that though, sure she could.

She was brought up in a different generation though. They were groomed as little girls to dote over their husbands and sacrifice themselves in service of their husbands.

I do plenty of doting myself but I refuse to sacrifice myself completely.

I believe we learn from prior generations.

We saw the moms before us and many of us silently agreed to not repeat the same patterns "when we grow up".

It's happening again right now. Moms will learn from their moms in every generation.

Generation X learned from the Baby Boomers, and the Gen Z's will learn from the Millennials. It's just what we do.

Things get passed down to the next, until the present generation says *"Nah, I don't like that. That doesn't work for me."* and they shake things up and do things differently. It's just the way it goes, especially in motherhood.

Now What??

1.) **Tune into your feelings**. Let discomfort and resentment be your guiding light. Be honest and ask yourself *"What's causing these feelings? What is it about this scenario, interaction, or person's expectation that's bothering me? Where in my life have I been unwilling to set boundaries?"* Recognize these uncomfortable feelings as a sign that you're pushing yourself beyond your own limits.

2.) **Own Your Limits**. Identify your physical, mental, emotional, and spiritual limits. What can you tolerate and accept and what can't you?

3.) **Give yourself permission**. Self-doubt, fear, and guilt are potential drawbacks. It's very easy to fear the other person's response to the boundaries we set. Always remember that setting boundaries are a sign of self-respect and a healthy relationship. Give yourself permission to not only set a standard of boundaries but to confidently stand up for them too.

Is Gratitude a Form of Self-Care?

Not many people would identify gratitude as a form of self-care…but the busy mom does.

Gratitude doesn't come easy but like any skill worth having, it requires practice.

It's easy to take things for granted and forget about all you have to be grateful for. When I was working at my full-time office job and running around like a mad woman trying to raise kids I envied the women who worked from home.

I complained that I was stuck working a nince-to-five and I painfully wished I could live her life. Eventually though, I realized envy and complaining wouldn't get me to the life I wanted to live.

Gratitude for the life I was *currently* living would, and that's exactly what happened.

I'm living the work from home life I so badly desired. But guess what---sometimes I take this for granted too. I'll admit that I even catch myself complaining now and again.

The truth is, there will <u>always</u> be something you wish was a little different. You'll constantly be chasing something. Maybe it's a new home, a job, or a new van because your family grew out of the small car you've been driving.

No matter what it is, it's really important to count your blessings on your way to the things you want. Mindfully appreciate what you currently have, who you currently are, and even what you currently weigh.

You can't afford to wait to be happy when you "get to where you want to be". Your life is happening now.

Don't let the negative things distract you from what you do have and what IS going right in your life.

Be grateful for the smallest of things and life will bring you more to be thankful for.

The bottom line is that there are 86,400 seconds in a day. Make sure one of them is used to simply say "Thank you" today.

Now What??

1.) *"My life is good today."* Write and/or repeat these words as you start out your day. It might feel fake and you might not yet believe them, but do it anyway.

2.) **Small reminders are everything.** When you notice you're starting to grumble about something that's stressing you or a negative event, jot down 3 or 4 related things that you're grateful for. I.e., when your partner does something to annoy you or he forgot to do something for you, write down a few things you *love* about him. If you're having rough days at work take a second to list a couple of reasons why you really like your job.

3.) **Keep a small gratitude notebook in your purse.** Scribble down all the reasons your life is *good* today. It might be the smallest of the smallest things. Maybe you're grateful for a sunny day after a few days of rain. Maybe it's for the necklace you're wearing because your grandmother gave it to you. Or maybe you're thankful for having a roof over your head or you appreciate your good health or supportive spouse/partner. Maybe you feel grateful for your delicious lunch. Just get the ball rolling and focus on gratitude more often.

How Can I Give Myself More Compassion?

Having lived in a downtown area, we often saw homeless people as we headed out for school, errands or dinner.

My heart broke for them every time. Many have weathered skin and dirty clothes. All too often when I walked by them, they didn't even bother to pick up their head to see me smiling at them.

They looked sad and lost. But at the same time, they seemed to be happy where they were. I often wondered how they got there or how long they've been homeless.

The details don't really matter though.

I tried to see beyond the exterior and treat each one with love and compassion.

When they asked for money, I gave what I could. Sometimes it was just a few bucks or even some loose change.

It's easy to have compassion towards homeless people, and the people we see suffering in the world.

I learned that one of my girlfriend's young

children was recently diagnosed with leukemia. My heart aches every time I read the social media updates about the procedures and his progress (or lack thereof).

For hours after reading the post I'll find myself thinking about what he and their entire family must be going through while simultaneously sending them love, strength and prayers. They weigh heavily on my heart.

The same thing happens when I read updates about someone losing their pet or a friend grieving the loss of a loved one.

I'm a highly sensitive empath, so I feel it *all*.

But you don't have to be an empath to feel compassion for others.

It's easy to have compassion for our kids, the people around us, and even strangers.

Activating self-compassion though, pssssh. That's an entirely different story. It's so much more difficult.

Take me for instance; one minute I'm feeling compassionate for a homeless person I don't even know, and the next minute I'm beating myself up for not writing a blog.

It's nuts.

Self-compassion is another topic that isn't usually

associated with self-care, but it is in fact a form of it.

In the early years of my self-care journey this was something I really struggled with.

I found though that one of the best ways to ignite the self-compassion within, is to treat yourself like you would a kid who wasn't feeling well.

Try to recall the last time your kiddo was sick.

Was it when he was burning up with a high fever?

Did she have a bad cold that kept her up coughing all night?

How about puking? Maybe your son puked all over the floor? Or was it the "*Hershey squirts*"?

Think back to the last time and bring to mind how awful they felt.

Maybe your daughter was so sick she couldn't even pick her head up from the pillow? Maybe your son couldn't talk because his throat hurt so badly?

What did you do? How did you react?

I'm willing to bet money that you treated your sick kiddo with kindness, love and compassion didn't you?

This past winter my son was really sick. Before the sun even came up he bolted for the toilet to throw up.

Unfortunately, he only made it to the bathroom sink.

It wasn't pretty.

Barely awake, I was up scooping chunks of last night's spinach dip out of the sink.

It was so gross and my stomach wasn't ready for all that so early in the morning. But I had one mission and that was to not let him see me gag. He kept apologizing and felt bad enough already. I didn't want him to feel any worse. It was easy to put his feelings in front of my own. I didn't even care I was scooping out puke, I was more concerned about the fact my son's peaceful sleep was abruptly interrupted.

I felt awful that he had to wake up that way and he felt so crappy. He just kept repeating *"No, no, no. I don't want to throw up anymore."* He tried fighting it, but his body won every time. He was absolutely miserable. He was burning up, achy and his stomach felt like it was turning inside out. He begged me to give him something that would make it stop and all I could do for him was shower him with so much love, comfort, and attention. For a full six days, I was by his side.

That's what moms do best, right? It just comes naturally.

What if we did the same for ourselves more often though?

When we found ourselves beating ourselves up for this and that, what if we soothed ourselves back to feeling better?

That's what self-care is about; learning to self-soothe ourselves.

Saying things like; *"It's OK. I'm doing my best. I'm a good person. I'm learning. It's alright. I love you. You're doing a good job. Everything is always working out for me. This isn't a huge deal. It's OK. I'm going to be ok. I'm not perfect, and that's ok."*

Sometimes I just stop and ask myself, *"Am I talking to myself like I would {insert best friend's name here} right now?"*

The answer is usually *"Hell no!"*

I would never put down or belittle my best friend, or *anyone* for that matter.

Asking myself this question helps to keep me in check. The way I choose to respond to myself usually changes quickly.

If my friend came to me for help because she was overwhelmed or frustrated about something, I'd be like *"Dude! You're being way too hard on yourself."*

If only you could see yourself through the eyes of a friend more often.

When I first started paying attention to my thoughts, I thought the goal was to get "rid" of that negative voice I had inside.

Boy was I wrong on that one.

I've learned that will never happen.

Our inner voice is a huge part of our human psyche and to some degree, we actually need that voice.

Our inner voice helps us make decisions, assemble logic and even calculates the best deals at the grocery store.

We depend on this inner voice.

But sometimes, maybe a little *too* much.

The goal isn't to shed that voice, but rather it's to not buy into *everything* that voice tells you.

If you listen closely to your inner voice, you'll see much of what it whispers to you is negative and possibly even downright nasty. Most of the inner chatter just replays stories of the past and worries about the future. Your aim is to refuse to believe them.

Once you're aware of this inner voice, then you can decipher what you <u>want</u> to believe. You can deliberately decide to let go of certain old beliefs that no longer serve you.

A huge secret to happiness is to learn how to see yourself through the eyes of love. This starts by changing your mind about who you claim yourself to be.

What if instead of judging and criticizing yourself, you accepted who you are in this very moment. It doesn't matter if you're twenty-pounds overweight or you haven't showered in days because you have a screaming infant and a toddler to attend to.

Surrendering to the place you're in doesn't mean you're giving up. This means you accept yourself while continuing to improve yourself. This means you honor where you are rather than trying to convince yourself you "should" be somewhere else.

You cannot get to where you want to go with hatred and self-loathing. Well, I suppose you technically could but the journey would be a long, tediously, ugly one.

You can decide today that the spaces between point A and point B are no longer going to be filled with self-hatred, guilt, and overwhelm. Replace these things with self-love, acceptance and self-care and you'll find your journey met with excitement and inner peace.

The other day, my husband was in a terrible mood; a flat-out pissy one. I finally got him to admit that it was because he felt there was a lack of time. He was slammed with work, he had to pick up my son and he felt like there was no time for it all to get done.

I explained to him (because he asked for my help) that this wasn't about a lack of time; this was about his lack of good thinking. His *perception* of the time and all the things he needed to get done was what led him to the bad mood in the first place. I challenged him and told him to go outside and take a few deep breaths for a bit. He said *"But I'm already lacking time, I can't do that."* I told him he didn't have time *not* to do that because this was about self-soothing himself, not about the time.

Still slightly stressed, he obliged.

When he came back in I suggested rather than working from his office desk that he grab his laptop and sit on the couch with his feet up.

I ran upstairs and grabbed his favorite blanket that his dad gave him and I threw it on top of him.

{Comfort ladies, it's all about comforting yourself.}

Within moments I saw his shoulders relax. I heard him take a deep breath and I watched him become calmer. I also witnessed him being one-hundred times more focused than before too.

He completed everything that he needed to get done and it wasn't done forcefully either. With his mind free from stress and negative thinking he ended up getting a lot more done because he had the headspace to think clearly. He neutralized his negative thoughts and this allowed him to focus on what was important.

I didn't create more time in the day for him; all I did was showed him the power of self-soothing compassion.

He still had the same amount of tasks to get done too. The only difference was the way he *approached* his tasks. Coming from a good space rather than a "lackful" one allowed him to shorten the amount of time it took to complete each one. He was operating from a place that served him (and his work) better.

Nurturing and forgiving yourself sets the stage for an overall better well-being. This can be experienced in your relationships, health and even your finances. There are tons of benefits of self-compassion and reduced levels of anxiety, overwhelm, and even depression are amongst a few of them.

Now What??

Take a second to think about how you usually treat yourself when you feel overwhelmed, make a mistake or fail to reach a goal you've set. If you have a habit of beating yourself up when things go wrong, start sprinkling self-compassion in your days.

1.) **Watch your language.** Criticizing yourself may

have become so normal that you don't even realize you're doing it. Pay close attention to the words you use to speak to yourself.

2.) **Give yourself encouragement**. Recognize when you're suffering and use kind words at these times. Think of what you'd say to a friend if she called you for support about a stressful situation; direct these similar compassionate responses toward yourself the next time you're faced with a difficulty.

3.) **Comfort your body**. Lie down and rest. Take a walk. Massage your own head, neck, or feet. Do anything to improve how you feel physically.

How Can I Stop Pushing Aside My Feelings?

A few months back, my oldest son who left the nest at eighteen asked if he could move back in a year later. On one hand, I was thrilled. Having gone through the experience of not having him at home for over a year, it made me realize how quickly they grow up.

There really is nothing like having my kids all under the same roof. It felt so weird not having them both at home. I found myself missing him a lot.

Then, on the other hand after he moved out, we downsized to an adorable little apartment in a downtown area of Florida.

We went from a suburban four-bedroom pool home to a two-bedroom apartment in a very short matter of time. It was no accident either; this was by design. It was right in alignment with our simplistic, minimalist lifestyle we were experimenting with. We got rid of *years* of "stuff" and traded it all in for life experiences such as road trips, new adventures, and making more memories to cherish rather than accumulating more stuff we didn't need. We started to really live our life by the design we created and the lifestyle we wanted.

Something inside my mom-head told me this was coming; I knew my son was about to ask to move back in. So I was *mostly* prepared.

When the day came and he moved all of his stuff into our tiny two-bedroom apartment though, things got real.

There was stuff *everywhere*. Dirty clothes, a mountain of laundry to be done, a new bed being set up, rearranged furniture ... I mean the place was in *total* disarray.

I felt like a sardine.

My youngest son traded in his queen sized-bed for a set of bunk beds. They were now sharing a room. Even when they were little they never had to share a room.

It wasn't the best set-up that's for sure. I knew it was only temporary and would have to do until we moved to a bigger place though.

We made numerous trips up and down the stairs unloading his things from my car.

Our front door was a very heavy one and it was set up to shut automatically. While I was in the bedroom dropping off the things I had in my hand I heard the door shut and what immediately followed was loud yelps from my dog.

I rushed to the door and realized my poor little dachshund's (Peanut) tail got caught in it. Thankfully it was just the tip of it.

My son had no idea how it happened because I didn't even get a chance to go over things and tell him about the front door yet.

Every time my poor dog moved his tail, blood splatted everywhere. He was freaking out and wouldn't let me touch it. By this point blood was flying across the room, all over the walls, all over us, and all over the floor. It was *not* a pretty sight.

I was finally able to pin Peanut down long enough to bandage it up.

It was a total shitshow really.

My son felt *awful*. Peanut was so busy following him and all the chaos around the house; he had no idea what hit him.

Welcome home buddy, *welcome home*!

I could've very easily had a major meltdown. But I didn't because thankfully, I had the tools to prepare me for days like this.

All I did was honor the feelings that were coming up.

I didn't try to beat myself up or shove down the

way I was feeling. I couldn't pretend I was something I wasn't.

I acknowledged I was overwhelmed and I let that be ok for now. I let whatever feelings came up to simply rise to the top.

I allowed my little controlling self to feel out of control.

I let myself be sad that we didn't have a spare room for my son at that moment.

And I didn't hide any of this from my family either. I just took lots of deep breaths, observed my feelings, and allowed them to pass through me. I flushed out several various emotions in the week of his arrival. I wasn't attached to any of them though.

Honoring our feelings certainly isn't always easy but our well-being is dependent on how we choose to honor or *dishonor* the way we feel in any given moment.

If we refuse to acknowledge the way we feel, we're really doing ourselves a disservice.

By honoring our own emotions, we're ultimately teaching our kids to honor theirs.

I don't want my boys to go through life

suppressing the way they feel. I want them to feel that it's OK to *feel* their feelings.

If they're sad, it's OK to cry. Crying is cleansing to the soul. We release what we need through our tears.

That's why we always feel better after a good cry.

When the lump in the throat disappears, that's a big indication of that. Ever notice how just before you open the flood gates, that lump just sits in the back of your throat, waiting. Waiting to be released.

That lump is the body's way of saying *"something needs to come out."*

It's no different with anger. Anger is natural and a basic human emotion.

If my kids are mad about something, I encourage them to punch a pillow if they need to.

If they're stressed, they can scream out the car window if they want.

It'd be foolish to tell my kids they aren't allowed to be mad or get angry. That's not only *unrealistic*, but suppression is toxic to our health.

So why not be the example and teach our kids how to work with their feelings by allowing ourselves to feel the way we do.

The good, the bad, the ugly.

Nobody wants to feel as though they "shouldn't" feel the way they do.

My husband and I have had this conversation many times over the years.

I *know* when I'm being a brat and in a funky mood. Internally I am *hyper-aware* of my thoughts and I instinctively have taught myself to work through them. I know myself well enough to know that once I just *accept* the fact that I'm in a bitchy mood and I stop trying to wish I wasn't, the funky mood dissolves.

It doesn't dissolve because I do nothing though. It dissolves because I cut myself some slack and allow myself to feel overwhelmed, sad, frustrated, etc. Once I do that, I soften. Once I soften, then I can activate my tools and try to do whatever I can to make myself happy again. I activate my self-care plan immediately.

Most of the time, that means I go for a walk. That's usually my go-to. Other times I meditate, do a yoga video, write, read a few pages of something inspirational, take a fifteen-minute nap, or relax in a hot bath.

I do whatever it takes to pull myself out of whatever funky feeling I'm experiencing. It doesn't matter what time of day it is or how many things I've got on my to-do list. If I want to be the best I can be and accomplish everything on my list and be there for my family, there is **nothing** more important than doing whatever it takes to shift my mood to one that serves me, and my family better.

The whole time though, I'm being kind to myself (or at least attempting to be). I'm not beating myself up for being in a bad mood, I just ask myself *"What do I need right now?"* And I go do it.

Most of the time, my husband doesn't even know I'm feeling funky. But once he does he usually goes into instant "fix-it" mode.

I love to hear his words of encouragement, the majority of the time.

But then there are times when I'm not the least bit receptive. When I'm in the midst of a total tantrum/pity party his "fix-it" words are like nails on a chalkboard. If I was a violent person, I'd just punch him in the face.

{POW!!}

Thankfully it's rare I get like that. But when I do ... my husband *hates* it. He admits what bothers him the most is that I'm unhappy and there's nothing he can do about it.

Even though it's just minutes or hours, he doesn't know what to do with himself.

I've explained to him that it's in those moments I need grace and a bit of extra love from him. Just a simple *"I'm sorry your morning went sideways, is there anything I can do?"*

I just want to feel validated. I want to feel assured that it's ok I feel the way that I do. If he tries to jam suggestions down my throat and I'm not ready for them, I'll flat out tell him *"I'm not there yet.*

The pity party won't last long; I know that about myself. I'll work through it, I always do. I refuse to put a time stamp on when my mood will improve in order to make my husband or anyone else feel more comfortable though.

Seeing someone in a bad mood sucks. It's uncomfortable.

Through time, grace, and space those negative feelings and that yucky mood will eventually melt away.

If this is what I want most for my kids, then I have to practice it when I'm faced with my own challenges.

I've spent too many years trying to push down the struggles of my life and the way I felt.

Sometimes I did it for the sake of family members; other times I did it because I couldn't bear to look at the painful situation in front of me. So I turned my cheek and tried to pretend it wasn't there.

In hindsight they both got me nowhere.

Now I see how unhealthy it was. Not just for myself but for everyone around me.

Dishonoring the way you feel shows up in loads of ways, but here are the most common:

1. You're sad but you tell the people around you that you're fine.

2. You're overwhelmed but you keep adding things to your plate

3. You're overwhelmed but you refuse to ask for help. If your partner asks if you need help you say *"I got it."*

4. You're annoyed and your partner asks you what's wrong and you say *"Nothing."*

5. You're exhausted but you refuse to sit for 2 minutes, take a power-nap, or go to bed early because *"there's too much to do"* or you fear you'll come across as "weak".

6. That lump in your throat isn't going away because you refuse to cry.

When you dishonor yourself, you not only wreak havoc on your body, but you also risk becoming unnecessarily resentful towards the people around you too; especially your partner or husband.

We have to remember the people around us aren't

mind readers. They don't know exactly how you feel, or why you're feeling a certain way. Only you do. Give yourself permission to feel the way you do when you do. Pretending you feel or don't feel a certain way may be a temporary Band-Aid to get through hard-times, but at some point you have to feel it in order to heal it.

Now What??

1. **Sit with a feeling and breathe**. When an emotion comes up, try not to fight to keep it down or resist it. Try relaxing and let yourself accept and feel whatever you feel instead. Allow yourself to fully experience feelings of stress, overwhelm, sadness, anger, pain, lack, or needing. By sitting with your feelings you're learning how to be more comfortable with them.

2. **Don't judge your emotions**. Resist the urge to label them. There are no "bad" emotions. Feelings are just feelings and all are acceptable. Witness them without judgement.

3. **Calm the feeling and** find ways to soothe it. Feel it, and then choose to let it go. Let empathy, self-compassion, and love follow.

How Do I Surrender?

"Peace requires us to release our illusions of control." ~ Jack Kornfield

Surrender means to let go, release, and give up. Not to give up trying, but to give up the *struggle*. Give up the resistance; to stop fighting.

It's in the sweet simplicity that we resist surrendering.

When we're trying to control, we're attached to an outcome. An outcome, *we* think is best.

When we surrender, we trust that no matter where our life leads us, no matter the outcome - somehow, someway - we will be ok no matter what.

In surrendering, we give up the need to micromanage the universe and the powerful force behind it.

When times get tough, we open ourselves up to new possibilities and we make it ok that a new path has been created on our behalf.

We have no idea what that "right" path is until we surrender.

Trying to control the people, the circumstances, and the outcomes of our lives is like paddling upstream.

It's as though we're in a canoe and instead of turning it downstream to go with the current of the waters, we turn it upstream and paddle as hard as we possibly can. The effort it takes to make it just a few feet is strenuous work. We make very little progress.

When we surrender, we turn our boat downstream and we let go of the oars. We allow ourselves to weave in and out of the natural flow of life; the river of life.

Too often after a long busy day, we finally lay our heads on our pillow. At last, we give ourselves permission to let the day be behind us. The cranky kids, the undone laundry, the bills, the traffic; we leave it all behind.

We settle down, relax and give ourselves the gift of rest and stillness to our minds.

We leave our troubles behind, close our eyes and slowly drift off to sleep.

The sun rises and as we open our eyes in the morning, we start stepping back into our minds. We begin recalling the circumstances of yesterday and all the things we laid aside just hours before.

Mindlessly, we begin to recount yesterday's

troubles. One by one they seep back into our mind.

We quickly trade the rest we allowed ourselves the night before for stress, fear, and worry.

We walk around in a bubble filled with all the things we're striving to control.

We falsely believe if we recall our worries, we're somehow "handling" them. We unwittingly convince ourselves that if we keep them at the forefront of our minds, then they'll be less likely to come true.

When in fact, this forces us to live in the very place we're trying to escape.

The more we allow worry to consume us, the more edgy and anxious we become. Its then we become more susceptible to sinking into a dark, powerless, and overwhelming place.

If daily we were to release the need for control and stop the obsessive worrying about the obstacles that may or may not reveal themselves, we would allow grace to enter our hearts.

The more we embrace and trust the journey the more life flows and the more joyful it becomes.

Rather than feeling fear of the unknown, feel curious and thrilled that something new is trying to materialize.

There will be phases of your life when everything feels like it's in chaos and conflict. It's in these moments though; you must remind yourself that a force beyond your awareness is reordering your life to match your heart's desires. It is bringing forth more of what you are calling from *within*.

Keep your faith and trust in life's process rather than waiting in fear. Sit back, relax and wholeheartedly trust that life's forces will carry you to where you're destined to be.

Trust and follow your hunches. Take inspired action and let go when you feel guided.

Surrendering doesn't mean you stop trying to create the best version of yourself or you give up in the face of difficulties. It means you let go of the grip these circumstances have over you; in your mind, body, and your soul.

Being open to allowing things to unfold is a skill that can be practiced. It's good to remind yourself that the universe is supporting you even when you don't think it is.

There's no need to worry, or attempt to micromanage the world around you.

Surrender to the beautiful mess you think your life is.

Now What?

1. **Ask.** When you're trying to control the very thing you can't, ask yourself this *"What am I so afraid of?"* Sometimes just shedding light on your worst fears can allow them to dissolve.

2. **Surrendering is not giving up**. You're accepting that the situation is happening while moving onto what you *could* do about it. {Fill in the blank} I accept that this is a stressful situation, and the way I could make it better is _____.

3. **Listen**. Your intuition is that voice that quietly guides you. This guidance comes from within the soul and is directly connected to the powers above. Listen to it and take action as you feel pulled to. Trust the voice within.

The Self-Care Practice

I mentioned previously that in order to implement self-care into your daily routine you first have to feel the value in it.

Once you know how valuable it is, not just to you, but to your entire family...you'll see that self-care isn't selfish and you'll practice it more often.

Self-care is about being true to yourself and doing things that put a smile on your face and lift you up.

You're learning how to flex those self-care muscles and how to take back your life through the art of self-care.

My goal is to help you put an end to the never-ending cycle of ignoring your own needs for the sake of everyone around you.

As a busy mom you may have bought into this thinking that there isn't enough time, money, or energy to put into self-care.

I get that!

You might catch yourself saying things like *"Once my kid(s) are _____, then I'll have time to take care of myself.* Or *"Once I have* _____, *it will be easier to do things for myself."*

These are lies though.

You don't need money, and a ton of time for self-care. This isn't about adding another thing onto your to-do list.

There's no real reason why you can't intentionally take care of yourself right from where you stand today. Those "reasons" are really just excuses.

They're excuses that will keep you away from what matters the most. There's likely a big part of your being that knows "you should" take care of yourself but you know it'll require you to get out of your comfort zone. These excuses are just your psyches way of keeping you "safe", and small.

It's a false sense of safety though.

Being a mom isn't always easy. The deep love we have for our kids drives us to putting them first.

If we can remember to just play around with the idea of self-care (alongside mom guilt and the many other blocks we feel) on a daily basis, we'll feel empowered.

My self-care practice looks nothing like it did when I started several years ago. It has changed immensely over the years. My kids were a lot younger when I first started, so in many ways my self-care practice has grown with them.

My regular self-care practice didn't happen overnight. So please, don't expect yours to either.

Like anything else - implementing self-care into our chaotic mom days takes practice.

Anytime we try something new, it always feels uncomfortable at first. Eventually though, that "new thing" becomes a habit.

So we have to stretch and exercise that muscle until self-care becomes as natural as brushing our teeth.

You will fail.

You will go back to your old ways.

You will forget about yourself, and you *will* put your needs on the back burner to serve others time and time again. You will become so depleted that you are forced to take care of yourself.

And then, you will begin again.

As a mom, the idea of putting yourself first may likely frighten you.

At the same time though, deep within there might be something that's drawing you towards it.

Even though it's taken me years to finally reach a point in my life that self-care is a natural part of every single day, I'm still learning and continuing to work on it. I'm always tweaking and fine-tuning my daily practice as I face life.

So start where you are.

You're not going to read this book once and become a self-care super mom.

In fact, chances are...you'll probably end up putting this book aside because life got busy.

I also know that one day you'll pick it up, and start again.

Self-care is something you pick away at; trying this one day, trying that another.

This is your self-care *practice*.

Something you will do over and over again until you acquire proficiency.

Remember, self-care is a way of honoring yourself *beyond* motherhood.

In the next few chapters I'll go over the four pillars of self-care. These will help you evaluate your own self-care practice, and help to create a daily dose of self-care and self-love.

S is for State of Mind.

E is for Energize.

L is for Lifestyle.

F is for Fun.

When all four pillars are being fed, you feel whole, and in alignment with the authentic nature of your true self. That is your main goal.

Pillar 1: <u>S</u> is for State of Mind

"Peace. It does not mean to be in a place where there is no noise, trouble or hard work. It means to be in the midst of those things and still be calm in your heart." ~ Unknown.

Self-care has to starts in the mind. Having a healthy state of mind is a matter of fully being present to the world around you. This doesn't mean just participating in life, this means to be present enough to really drink life up.

Our state of mind plays a huge role in our self-care practice. In fact, it's the main event. It's our state of mind and belief systems that determines and drives the actions we take.

The moods we're in, how we react to something our kid just did, and how we treat our partners is largely dependent on our inner state of mind.

If your mind is right, you can handle anything.

The first order of business is how you're viewing self-care. If your outlook is that self-care is *impossible*, then the result you get will be an impossible one.

If however, you're approaching the idea of adding self-care into your life as a possibility and you're willing to get curious about it, you will achieve the outcome you desire.

You have to really feel you deserve the same love and attention you give to your kids and family. You must start there.

If you don't already have a *"the glass is half full"* mentality, start adopting one now. At least begin to feel the *possibility* of that. Imagine living in a world (your inner world) where you sought the solutions and answers rather than focusing on what's missing and the impossibility of the things in front of you.

"Where do I start?" was the question I asked myself over and over when I first began my own self-care journey. It's the question I most often get asked by women too.

When I first started asking myself that question, I'd get annoyed because coming up with an answer was hard. *"Where the %$#@ do I begin? Why can't someone just give me the answer! Why does this have to be so hard!?"*

I'd always come back and try to answer it though. I became obsessed with this question.

"Where do I start?"

I don't know how, but I knew deep down self-care

was the way to inner peace and true happiness and <u>that</u> was what I was ultimately after. I needed calm. I craved peace.

I finally got to a point where I stopped asking the question and I just started taking action.

I played around with the idea of self-care at first. I dabbled.

I knew I had to just start where I was.

Then the big fat HOW came into play.

If self-care was about doing more things I loved to do, <u>*how*</u> in the world would I find the time to do them? The time to write the book I always wanted to write, or meditate, meet with girlfriends, read, exercise, and just simply slow down and enjoy the food in front of me?

These questions burned in my mind every day. They haunted me at night as I tried to go to sleep because I was so desperate for change.

I knew there was an answer and I wasn't going to stop until I found it. The pain of where I was in my life became far too great for me to ignore anymore.

I had enough.

I knew there was more to me. Even though I couldn't pinpoint it, I felt utterly disconnected from myself. I wanted so badly to feel whole again.

Finally, one day the answer hit me.

{Drum roll please...}

It's not about finding the time to do these things; it's about <u>making</u> the time to do them.

Woah! What a groundbreaking concept!

So simple, yet so damn complicated for the busy mom.

I began finding small ways to take care of <u>me</u>.

I found that it was the small things that added up to the big things. Something so little as taking my vitamins or washing off my makeup and applying face cream before I went to bed made me feel more human, more whole.

Some days I had to push myself to do something for <u>me</u>. It felt unnatural and awkward at first.

It felt like doing anything for me went against every grain in my body.

I was so far out of my comfort zone.

I knew though, that there were moms out there with four or five kids still meeting their friends for monthly lunches and attending weekly kick boxing classes.

They had the same exact amount of time in a day that I had and they made it work.

"But I'm a single mom. They probably have a husband to help them. I don't."

That was one of my favorite excuses.

I knew damn well that was a bunch of bull too. There were moms who had even *less* support than I had. At least I had my mom who lived just a few miles down the road to call on if I needed. Some single moms didn't even have that.

This is why self-care starts in the mind. It's a matter of being mindfully aware of all those thoughts that try to keep us away from nurturing ourselves and taking good care of ourselves.

Time to yourself is an *investment*.

You would never knowingly invest in something you didn't think was going to give you a good return, would you?

The goal is to start to reframe your thinking so you get onboard with the idea that taking time out for yourself doesn't take away from your kids or anyone else around you.

If it makes you feel better and if it uplifts your mood, then it's an <u>investment</u> of your time. It adds VALUE.

Self-care is an <u>investment</u> of my time.

Self-care is an <u>investment</u> of my time.

Self-care is an <u>investment</u> of my time.

That's not a typo. I wrote it three times.

Let those words marinate in your head like the chicken in your fridge.

Roll them around and replay them over and over in your mind until you *know* them. Not intellectually, but you really know them to be true.

Say them randomly throughout your day until it "clicks".

Right now, the idea of time to yourself being an investment might feel very foreign to you. It's not what we're taught in society or even in our families.

Sadly, we're taught that doing things for ourselves is selfish because it takes <u>away</u> from family time.

Circling back to my mom living down the street from me…even though I could technically call on her whenever I needed her, I rarely did.

The shared custody order between my ex-husband and I was set up so that I had the kids four out of the five days during the week and we alternated weekends.

In the court's eyes, in my eyes, in my ex's eyes...I had them mostly during the week. So *"what kind of mother would I be if I let my mom take them after school one day a week?"*

That's how deeply ingrained the idea of self-care being a selfish act was for me.

I was still pretty bitter and felt bad that because of the divorce I saw my kids less than most moms. I wanted to have them all the time like a *"normal family"*.

At the same time...I needed a freaking break! Being a mom is hard. Being a single mom was no joke.

So, on Wednesday afternoons my mom would pick up both boys from their separate schools. She'd bring them to her house, order pizza, and then drop them back off to me just before their bedtime.

They were both already bathed and showered too.

It was heaven.

It felt so weird to be able to leave work unhurried and then go straight home. I didn't even know what to do with myself. I felt like I was forgetting something.

Sometimes I would think about meeting a girlfriend out for a quick drink. Most of the time I was so exhausted all I wanted to do was go home though.

Should I take a long hot uninterrupted bubble bath? A

shower? Maybe I should clean the house. Should I do some writing? Maybe I should curl up on the couch with my dog and read a couple pages of a book. Maybe I could watch that show I've wanted to watch. Or call my friend? I should probably eat something. What should I cook though? For just one person? That's weird.

I was so lost. I would just spin my wheels and end up doing nothing.

I literally didn't know what to do with myself.

That was a problem.

If I wasn't putting out fires, cleaning, up messes, or taking care of little humans I didn't feel right.

I was always in this constant state of chaos and I think a part of me liked that.

I fed off it.

I have a high energy personality, so I did everything fast back then. I drove fast, I walked fast, I ate fast, I showered fast, I got ready fast, and I always had a zillion thoughts zipping through my head - I was always on the go. Internally and externally.

I never stopped. When I tried to, I wanted to come out of my skin because it felt so unnatural to me.

Doing "nothing" made me feel anxious. There seemed to be this invisible pull to get up and do *something*, **anything**. I felt a mountain of guilt if I wasn't busy.

As each Wednesday approached, I would start thinking about what I wanted to do. How would I best take advantage of this free time?

There was always a mile-long list.

So much to do, and so little time.

No matter what I ended up doing (or NOT doing), or how uncomfortable it felt, I always felt recharged when the boys returned though.

The mom the boys came home to from Nana's house was a different mom than the rest of the week mom they got.

The difference was palpable.

I was way more calm and in the present moment. On Wednesdays I found myself seeing the boys with a fresh set of eyes; my heart was full of deep appreciation and love. I felt calm and relaxed.

"Why couldn't it be this way when I had the kids?" I wondered.

I was fascinated and curious.

Why was I putting so much pressure on myself? There had to be a way for me to feel this chill while the kids were home?

Why couldn't I just forget about time and loosen the reigns on structure a bit?

Sure, the kids still needed to get to bed by eight o'clock. But at the same time, the bedtime police weren't going to come in and take my kids away if they got to bed fifteen minutes later than usual.

<u>I</u> was the bedtime police. There were no outside forces; I was the only one putting all this crazy pressure on myself.

I knew they'd still get to bed at a decent hour.

I realized I could still be present and get everything done on time too.

Just maybe act less like a drill sergeant though and more like a loving, present mom.

<u>Now What??</u>

1. Write these words down and post them on your bathroom mirror or set an alarm in your phone to go off a couple of times a day. *"Self-care is an <u>investment</u> of my time."*

2. Approach your day with a caring, nurturing, unhurried mentality. The things you need to get done will be accomplished more efficiently when you have a calm mind.

How Can I Quiet My Racing Mind?

I was a tough cookie and strong in so many ways, but when it came to my self-care, I played the powerless victim.

"I have no time."

"My kids need me."

"I'm a mom."

It was always something. Some excuse. Something to keep me away from myself.

It wasn't about changing my past or about changing my kids' age, or even their behavior. It wasn't about my career and long work hours, and it certainly wasn't about any other outside circumstances.

This had to be an inside job. It had to start with me.

All I really needed was a willingness to consume small fun sized bites of self-care.

Meditation was something I wanted to incorporate into my self-care practice, but I was super intimidated by the word itself. This is why I called it "quieting my mind" or "sitting still" instead.

Just sitting quietly for a few minutes every day has allowed the answers of my life's big questions to be revealed to me. Step after step I've been guided to the next. Like little gumdrops on the path of life. My only job has been to get quiet, listen, and honor the guidance with every unknown step.

I had to redesign my life from the inside out.

I could see that for a long time there was a piece of me that was still running; running from the stillness and the silence. Sure, I was legit busy, but in reality what I was *really* doing was hiding from myself.

Like I said, I was a busy body and an expert at keeping myself busy. I never sat. The idea of being "present" and bringing mindfulness into my life was stressful in the beginning.

I found in the early days of my poor attempts to be quiet and still, my inner self-loathing diva would rear her ugly little head and say things like *"You suck. You're a bad mom. You don't do enough. Your dad abandoned you. Your step-dad hates you because you're a loser. Get up and do something productive. Your ex-husband cheated on you because you weren't good enough. You suck at relationships. You're a failure because you had a kid at such a young age..."*

Blah, blah, blah.

The baggage of my past felt like a volcano

bubbling up to the surface every time I would try to quiet my mind. It did the opposite of quieting; it **screamed** ugly, nasty shit at me instead.

If it wasn't shrieking offensively at me, then it was running off a long list of things I needed to be doing. Like laundry, the grocery shopping and cleaning the disorganized garage.

It was insanity.

Eventually though, I learned to get quiet by just seeing the obnoxious thoughts float by like a balloon in the air. I refrained from dwelling in them.

I stopped believing everything that voice was saying too.

I started challenging all the old beliefs that made me feel like utter shit about myself.

"You suck. You're a bad mom." Actually, that's not true…I'm not perfect, but I'm pretty damn awesome.

"You don't do enough." I do plenty. And I'm enough regardless of how much I do or don't do.

"Your dad abandoned you." His suicide wasn't about me; it was about him.

"Your step-dad hates you because you're a loser." He hates everyone. His opinion means nothing.

"Get up and do something productive." I'm quieting

the mind, that's the most productive thing I can do for myself.

"Your ex-husband cheated on you because you weren't good enough." He cheated on me because he was insecure and his self-worth needed to be filled by a woman outside of our marriage in order to feel good about himself.

"You suck at relationships." That's no longer my story. I've improved in so many awesome ways.

"You're a failure because you had a kid at such a young age…" Actually, I was brave and courageous. Having him made me a better person.

What I was doing was consciously choosing to bring those dark parts of myself into the light. I sat with them rather than trying to avoid them the way I've done in the past.

Meditation is a mind tool that will help you get through your difficult days of being a mom and all the demands you face. I knew about meditation years before I actually started practicing it but because I was super intimidated by it I avoided it. When the pain of my racing thoughts and unease became too great, I decided to finally give it a go.

Calling it "sitting still" or "quieting my mind" felt easier, more doable. I think it was because the word meditation has all of these other things attached to it.

Like sitting in a certain position, and holding my fingers in a certain way.

Screw all that nonsense. I needed simple.

I knew I had to start small and not place high expectations on myself; at least at first anyway. I began by playing a game with myself. I'd set the timer for one-minute to see if I could just sit still without fidgeting. Remember, I was a busy-body so sitting still was a huge challenge in itself, never mind trying to quiet the mind too. The first several times I fidgeted like a toddler with a full bladder and my thoughts raced. I spent most of my time thinking rather than enjoying the "non-thought".

I had zero concept of what "non-thought" even was back then. After a couple of weeks of playing this game I noticed sitting got easier. I increased my time to five-minutes. Now that I was feeling more comfortable with sitting, my goal now was to quiet my thoughts…or so I thought. When I first tried this, my thoughts were continually tossed around. In an attempt to force myself into silence, I tried to fight through the thoughts that spun in my head. (My mind was a rowdy raging little bugger.)

The more we fight against this though, the tougher meditation and sitting quietly is. I've learned that it's useless to become annoyed and frustrated when the mind persists with thought. It's just doing what it does best. Once I stopped fighting against it and simply allowed it to flow naturally, I began to step into the depths of my inner self beyond all the chaos.

I *allowed* the thoughts to come and go. Like the waves in the ocean I just witnessed them. I stopped dwelling and analyzing them and instead I just let them float by.

Letting my thoughts arise rather than fight them helped to put them at ease. I noticed once I gave myself permission to have these racing thoughts, they quieted.

The more I was willing to practice, the easier meditating became. I've been practicing meditation consistently for over eight years now and it's become a big part of my daily routine. Never in a million years did I think I would experience a quiet mind within the first two seconds on a good day and the first couple minutes on a "bad" one. More often, I can easily let go of it all. I used to need complete silence or a guided meditation to achieve the peace I was after but nowadays I can have my eyes opened or closed in a noisy doctor's office and meditate quietly. It might not be a deep one, but it's just enough to re-center myself.

Meditating is a busy mom's lifeline.

The powerful beauty of it doesn't only last while you're sitting there either. The benefits of a morning meditation will carry you through your day. You'll find that even though you still have the same busy tasks and chaos, the way you approach them is from a calmer and more peaceful place.

You'll feel less overwhelmed and you won't feel like you're on such an emotional roller coaster. Things seem to get done easier, you'll feel like there's more time in your day and you're so much less reactive to the craziness around you.

Like every other self-care activity, meditation or sitting quietly for a few minutes every day ultimately makes you a better mom.

Now What??

1. **Start where you are**. Don't expect too much from yourself in the beginning. Refuse to get caught up in the process, like how you should be sitting or holding your fingers. If you feel like sitting, sit. If you feel like lying on your back, then do that.

2. **Start small**. Set the timer for 2-3 minutes every day for 21 days and see if you can just sit still. The amount of time isn't as important as it is to just giving yourself a few minutes of quiet time each and every day.

3. **Witness your thoughts**. Don't try to analyze or figure out your problems. Just watch your thoughts float by like a balloon.

4. **Increase your time every week**. Incrementally up the amount of time you're sitting. Do this as you feel comfortable and work at your own pace.

5. **Don't hide meditation from your kids.** Meditate in front of them sometimes. If they crawl all over you, let them. But continue to keep your eyes shut and be still. Eventually they may want to imitate you. Be the example and let them see the healthy benefits of sitting quietly.

Do The Thoughts I Think Really Matter?

"If you are depressed you are living in the past.

If you are anxious you are living in the future.

If you are at peace you are living in the present."

— *Lao Tzu*

The other morning, while I was in the shower - at 5:30a.m. - I caught myself having full blown, drawn out conversations with myself.

I was already mapping out new things for my coaching client and listing out all the stuff my son needed to bring to his track practice...which was at 4 PM!!

NEARLY 12 HOURS LATER.

As soon as I realized what I was doing, I stopped. I took a big, deep breath and reminded myself that none of that stuff mattered right now. None of it.

My only job was to just enjoy my shower.

That was all.

Instantly, my breathing slowed.

My mind stopped racing and my shoulders dropped as I began to pay attention to the warm water hitting my back.

That was all it took.

I don't think we'll ever stop having this constant chatter in our heads.

The mind is what makes us great.

But we don't have to let our minds be in the driver's seat all the time.

Just like the mom-guilt, it's so important to kick it out every once in a while.

Learning to quiet our minds is the key to inner peace.

Redirecting our mind rather than just letting it have its ways with us is what will help us feel calm.

It's hard to do this if you're unaware of the chatter that's babbling in the background of your mind.

Challenge the thoughts and don't believe everything you tell yourself. Awareness is huge. Before you can redirect your thoughts, you have to be aware and able to really listen to yourself.

Thoughts are going to happen but the more you can quiet your mind, the calmer you'll feel.

Today, just be aware of the conversations you're having with yourself.

Notice your thoughts while you're driving, brushing your teeth, or cleaning the dirty dishes.

The mindless activities are usually what trigger the thoughts to zip ninety-miles-an-hour.

If the thoughts are kind and loving and its saying things like *"I'm beautiful, I'm awesome"*, and then honor them.

If they're ugly thoughts like *"I suck, I'm a slacker, and I'm fat…"*

Release them with love.

Letting our thoughts run wild is what leads us to feeling tired, overwhelmed, and feeling depleted.

In the middle of the day a few days ago, I caught myself starting to rattle off all the things I haven't done yet. Like make my oldest son new house keys, hang the pictures on the wall, clean out the hall closet and change our address at the vet's office.

As soon as I heard myself, I stopped.

Instead of going down that rabbit hole, I began to recall all the things I DID accomplish.

Which were: edit my book, chat with my youngest, help a coaching client, make my husband's lunch, and help my man-child return a piece of crap car that he bought from a car dealer.

Now --- I think <u>those</u> things are much bigger and way more important in the bigger picture of life. Don't you? I mean really, how silly is it to stress about not cleaning the hall closet when I just helped a coaching client and then helped my son get his money back.

Those are huge things.

As busy moms though, we tend to minimize the things we do. Day after day, we get so caught up with everything we don't get done and we lose sight of the really important things we accomplish.

By accomplish, I don't necessarily mean *"doing"* either, it can mean *"being"*. For example, me chatting with my son wasn't really "accomplishing" anything in the sense of doing...but I was *being* present for my child.

See the difference?

My point is, it's not always the doing things that are important. Sometimes the most important thing you can *do* is not anything at all. You could be tending to a sick child, or putting a Band-Aid on your son's skinned up knee but you haven't emptied the dishwasher or folded laundry yet.

You *being* there for your child is way more important than the dishes and clothes, right?

We know this intellectually, but as busy moms it's easy to forget and it's even easier to start beating ourselves up.

Simply being fully present might be the single most important thing you can do for yourself, your kids, and your family.

So the next time your mind wants to focus on all the things you haven't done yet, turn your eyes towards all the things you did get done and refuse to minimize the importance of them. Don't allow your mind to take control and spin off into negativity.

Redirect it. You have the ability to do that. This is the beauty of our minds. We can choose what we think.

Now What??

1.   **Take note.** Pay attention to your thoughts today, especially as you do those mindless activities.

2.   **Change the language**. If you find that you're often berating yourself, choose a more positive thought. Your past doesn't have to define your future. Rewrite the script. After all, you're the one telling the story.

Pillar 2: <u>E</u> is for Energize

Is Exercise Really That Important?

I find it funny that I'm putting this in my book since I was anti-working out for years and years. I "hated" exercise. I dreamt about being that girl who woke up in the morning and looked forward to going to the gym and being all sweaty, and toned. I've bought countless gym memberships that I never even ended up using. I'd buy it all amped up and determined to use it at least three to four times a week. I'd even go through my trainer appointments to learn how to use the machines.

I'd wake up so excited and listen to my favorite music on the way to the gym. I'd walk in, look around at the machines trying to decide where I'd start first, and I'd head straight for the treadmill. Every single time. So basically I paid a monthly membership fee to walk nowhere, while indoors.

I did that for years, trying to shove myself into a box I clearly didn't belong in.

I knew my self-care practice had to include ways of moving my body but I had no idea what I wanted that to look like yet.

The only things I really knew were that I wanted it

to be fun, I wanted to love it, and I hoped to gain new friendships from it. I wanted to feel that sense of camaraderie.

The idea of simply "moving my body" felt way better than the word "exercise".

So, I Googled *"fun exercise classes"* and the first one that popped up in my city was a boot camp style class right by the bay where I lived. I read through tons of reviews and many of them said *"I love the variety of exercises we do and the view is absolutely gorgeous."* Bingo! That's what I craved. Variety. The view was a bonus. I signed up for my first free class and was addicted. It was exactly what I *wanted*.

I've learned that the key to me exercising on a regular basis isn't about forcing myself to do something everyone else does; it's about finding ways to move my body that I *enjoy*.

In this current season of my life, I no longer do the boot camp style exercise. My body began craving something different after I injured my neck and shoulder. I desired more gentle ways of moving my body.

Listening to my body has become more important than anything else. On a daily basis I ask myself, *"How do I feel like moving my body today?"* I let it tell me. I listen to what my body needs. Somedays I feel like jumping online to do a Pilates video. Then there are days I feel like doing yoga. There are other days that all I want to do is hop on my bike and go for a bike ride. Sometimes a walk or light jog is appealing.

I've stopped trying to shove myself into these boxes my body doesn't want to be in.

My main objective is to just move my body every single day.

<u>Now What??</u>

1.) **Start where you are**. Don't expect yourself to run a marathon if you haven't been running. Take your time and enjoy the process of moving your body.

2.) **Find exercises you really enjoy doing**. If you get bored easily (like me), know you can switch it up anytime.

3.) **Do them**. Once you find something you like, be brave and sign up and go do it.

Jody Agard

What Does Eating Have to Do with Self-Care?

I've been asked *"What does eating have to do with self-care?"* so many times! I used to wonder the same thing too. For a long time I didn't see the connection either. What I've learned though is that when we take care of ourselves from the inside first, it's easy to take care of our outside. The foods we put into our body is no different. When it comes to eating, I try to approach it the same way I do moving my body, and life; in a loving, gentle way. My body knows what it needs and wants, but it's up to me to listen and honor it.

I have to be the one who decides how to nourish this vehicle I'm in. I've become very aware of how I feel after I eat certain foods. If I go for two, or three, or four slices of pizza, I know I'll pay the price for how I feel later. Sometimes I'll do it anyway. Other times I only eat one slice just to satisfy my pizza craving because it's not worth feeling tired, bloated, and crappy later. Same goes with sweets. I love my sweets. They don't come without a price though. If I eat too many, I get a huge headache. Sometimes it's worth it, most of the time it's not.

My body has become extra sensitive to sugar intake these last few years so I try to let that guide me. I have to ask myself *"Is eating this entire bag of candy worth a headache later?"* Most of the time the answer is no, but there are definitely times the consequences feel worth it in that moment.

For me, it's not about the numbers on the scale anymore. Its more about how I feel. I want to live my life feeling the best I can. I know when I eat too much or don't fit in some of my clothes; I don't feel good about myself. Not feeling good about myself affects everything in my life; my confidence, my self-worth, my sex drive, and my energy levels. I know these things all play into what kind of mood I'm in, which translates to how I show up to my family, my clients, and this beautiful planet I live. If what I'm ultimately after is to operate at my highest potential, I have to be conscious of this stuff.

For me, it's not always about what I'm missing out on. I.e. sweets, pizza, etc....it's more about what I'll be gaining. The ways you choose to energize your body is completely up to you. Just know that when you decide to feed your body with whole foods, you're not only nourishing your body, you're nourishing your mind too.

Self-care and energizing your body is about truly caring for yourself and doing your best to treat your body with the same love and respect as you would give to your child.

You deserve that.

<u>Now What??</u>

1. **Eat more foods that fuel you.** Try to find healthy versions of the things you like. Start sprinkling them into your weekly meals. It doesn't have to be every meal. Start small. I.e. Zucchini noodles instead of spaghetti sometimes. Turkey meat instead of beef. Whole grain pastas instead of the white pastas.

2. **Allow yourself to splurge.** If you want pizza, eat it. If you want ice cream, eat that too. Don't feel guilty about it. This will only make you feel worse about yourself which will likely make you want to throw in the towel. Give yourself permission to let your diet evolve and in the process, enjoy the foods you love without the guilt.

Is Sleep Really a Form of Self-Care?

Have you ever been to Italy?

I haven't. It's on my bucket list though. I heard they take "Siestas".

Between the hours of 1 and 4 pm apparently you'll find shops, churches, and museums closed so that owners can go home and take a nap or enjoy a long lunch. The Italians aren't the only ones doing it either. Countries like Greece, the Philippines, Costa Rica, Mexico, Ecuador, and Nigeria are known to participate too. I think they're on to something.

You need sleep to function. This is a no brainer. Be willing to rest when you're tired. Give yourself permission to recharge your batteries if you get sleepy. Who cares that you still have laundry to do. Lay down with the kiddo or set your timer for 20 minutes and take a power nap.

Closing your eyes for a few will boost your willpower, memory and productivity. It'll help to enhance your creativity, and calm your nerves too. I've seen this time and time again in my own life. The hard part isn't falling asleep as much as it is giving yourself permission to close your eyes. If you can get through that, you'll be rewarded with a ton of energy.

Now What?

Although exercise, eating, and sleeping are the main components of pillar 2, there are several other ways to energize your mind, body, and soul too. I'll rattle some of my favorite off below.

1. Bring the aroma of essential oils into your home

2. Take a walk. The more time you can spend in nature, the more energized you'll feel. Visit a local park, hike some trails or just take a quick walk around your neighborhood.

3. Feed your creative side. Color, paint, or write (you don't have to share it with anyone). Do something that activates the right side of your brain.

4. Escape into a good book. You've heard the saying before *"readers are leaders."* Be a leader. If you want your kids to read, be the example and give yourself permission to snuggle up with a good book.

5. Meditate or practice mindfulness. Give yourself a few minutes to center your breathing and quiet your mind.

6. Stretch. Take a moment each morning to stretch. Reach for the sky, bend to touch the ground, take deep breaths and stretch your body. Get up from your desk and gently stretch throughout the day.

7. Drink water. We're no different than the flower

needing water. Instead of drinking a midday energy drink, slam a big glass of water with lemon in it and watch how energized you feel.

8. Conscious breathing: Pause in between your hectic schedule and make a conscious effort to breathe deeply. In through your nose, out through your mouth. Repeat 3 times. You can do this one while sitting at your desk.

9. Listen to calm, soothing music or inspiring audios that help to induce a calm state.

Pillar 3: L is for Lifestyle

"If you don't design your own life plan, chances are you'll fall into someone else's plan. And guess what they have planned for you? Not much." Jim Rohn

Happiness is living a life you don't want to escape from.

Over the course of my mom journey, I'll admit that I've had thoughts like *"I need a fucking drink!* more times than I'd like to admit. I sometimes wondered what it would be like if instead of heading to carline to grab the kiddo; what if I just kept driving and ran away. I'd daydream about sitting on the beach somewhere with no responsibilities, no demands, and nobody screaming "Mom!"

I'd also dream about hiding in my bed under the covers and not dealing with any of my life stressors. Then there were times in my life that I've done just that. Hid under the covers that is, not run away.

In those moments, it was never really about my kids and this certainly didn't have anything to do with the love I have for them either. In those desperate moments, it was about me feeling overwhelmed with life.

The best thing about life though, is that we are in

charge of it.

Thankfully we live in a country where we are free to choose how we live.

If you look at your own life up until this very moment…out of your own free will you got to decide who your partner/husband would be, what city you live, what house to buy or rent, and what career path to take. You get to decide what foods to eat and how to discipline your kids too.

These are all *your* choices.

Sometimes though, we fall into a rut of living a life we no longer enjoy. Paralyzed with comfort and fear, we continue to live it anyway.

Working many years in a full-time job, I adopted this belief that working for someone else was the only path to stability and therefore happiness. For years I believed that I had no other choice then to get up and work the hamster wheel of the nine-to-five job.

Until, that is - wanting *something more and* something *different* began to pull at my heart strings.

This "tugging" in my heart was just there. It was an unsettling feeling because I couldn't control it. A part of me wished I was still happy doing what I was doing, so I tried to ignore it for as long as I could. There came a day though that I could no longer deny it. I knew I had to trust and honor it.

I had no idea what I was going to do next. All I knew was that I wanted to positively impact the world in a bigger way; I wanted to make a *difference*. I also wanted to work from home. I wanted to build my career around the lifestyle I wanted to live instead of the other way around. I craved the freedom to create my own schedule and to work for myself. I wanted the freedom to volunteer at my kid's school in the middle of the day if that's what I wanted to do.

I wanted to not feel bad if one of my boys was sick and couldn't go to school. I wanted to be able to stay home with them and snuggle them on the couch, and not have to worry about calling in and disappointing my boss. I wanted the ability to work from a coffee shop every now and then.

I wanted to wake up and meditate, write blogs, books, and record videos. I wanted to coach clients and be that person in their life empowering them with tools that would change their life. I wanted to do workshops and speak in front of audiences (even though the thought of it made me want to poo my pants.)I wanted to be surrounded by positive, inspiring people who believed in me. I wanted to feel unhurried and not race through life. I wanted time in the morning to quietly sip my coffee in peace and set my intentions for the day.

At the time however, I was *far* from living that life. This didn't stop me from dreaming about it or believing that one day I could have it though. It simply meant that my daily activities had to involve taking steps towards all of the things I wanted in the future. I knew this wouldn't happen overnight, and I just had to pick away at it.

I was downright scared. I can't even put into words how scared I was.

I took steps with fear screaming in my face anyway though. I had to. The pain of living the comfortable life I'd been living became too big for me to ignore. I was also being pulled by a vision – to be an author, a coach, and sharing my message of self-care and self-love to anyone who would listen.

After I declared what I wanted and once I began to take daily action towards my dreams there was a huge period of CHANGE (and uncertainty). I felt like a baby walking for the first time.

I was so unsteady.

My entire life went through an upheaval process. The dynamics of my relationships changed. Who I hung out with changed. The way I communicated changed. The foods I ate changed. The books I read changed. How I spent my weekends changed. The number of things I said yes to dropped dramatically because I got pickier about how I chose to spend my time. And I started asking for more help from my family too.

I could go on and on.

I would be lying if I said it wasn't uncomfortable, it was. At the same time though, it made me feel more alive than ever. So I tried to keep my eyes on that part of it.

If you're currently living a life that no longer gives you joy, you have the freedom to change it.

Sure, at first it might not be easy but in the end you'll find that it's so worth it.

Change requires us to form new habits, which is why it's easy to avoid it.

It's said that change often comes when we are either *pushed* by pain or *pulled* by a dream or vision.

When you're pushed by pain it means your life circumstances are screaming at you. The pain of what's in front of you is essentially **forcing** you to look at things in ways you likely haven't been open to in the past. Deep down there might be a big part of you that knows you can't continue to live the way you have been. Maybe you received an unexpected health diagnosis, your marriage is starting to crumble, or you're just simply unhappy.

If in the area of health, relationships, career or finances you're experiencing a great deal of discontent then let that serve as an alarm to do something about it.

What that feeling of discontent is saying to you is that there's something out of alignment with the truth of who you are. There's something out of whack.

The sadness, the worry, the arguments, the anxiety, the stress…these emotions are *pushing* you to make changes. If you continue to ignore the initial whispers, the pain of your unhappiness will begin to squawk. Loudly.

Being pulled by a dream or vision is different though. In this case you may have dreams about starting your own business, starting an online store so you can sell all your cool crafts, or staying at home to raise your kids. You might have all these ideas and they won't leave you alone. But you come up with millions of different reasons why you can't take steps towards them. The dream or vision haunts you and you might not be able to stop thinking about it. That's because you're being nudged by something much bigger than yourself. You're being called to step outside your comfort zone and design the life you *want*.

Getting out of your comfort zone, doing things that scare you, and chasing dreams is no walk in the park.

For me, following my heart and changing my life has probably been one of the most difficult things I've ever done. Because of small changes over a long period of time, today I sit inside the dream that felt impossible. Many of the things I craved, I fulfilled. Some, I haven't and am still working towards. I'm also working on new stuff too. New dreams, new things that scare the hell out of me, new ways to leap out of my comfort zone, and new ways of self-caring.

Be willing to rock the boat in service of where you truly want to go.

Your family members, friends and loved ones won't always understand the "new you". Many of them might tell you *"You've changed; I want the old {insert name here} back."* Friends might even joke *"You used to be so much more fun."*

I had a client *"Emma"* once. She was a mom in her early thirties with three kids under the age of eight years old. Her health had been failing her, the number of anxiety attacks and her levels of stress became way too much for her to handle by herself. She tried to put herself first but her husband was having a really hard time with it. During our first coaching session I asked her to give me a rundown of her daily schedule. She explained that her husband was a really great dad, but she wished he was half the husband that he was a father. Emma worked full-time; she did all of the cooking, the cleaning, the laundry, the kids homework, the kids drop off and pick-ups from school and doctor appointments.

Her husband worked, and came home every day to a clean house and an already prepared meal. All he needed to do was shower, eat, get his clothes ready for the next day, and take the dog out.

"That's all he does! I do all the rest Jody! He has it made!"

I replied "Yes, you've made his life very easy."

"Yeah I have. But how do I un-do what I've done though? It feels like every time I ask for help he complains."

I explained to her that she needed to be willing to rock that boat a bit. *"It's not going to be comfortable, and you guys may even hit some rough seas and have some arguments over the new way you're doing things, but it will be worth it. Own up to the fact that you need help. Really own that. Stand up for what you want. It'll take time for everyone to adjust but things will eventually settle."*

We had been working together for a few weeks when one evening I got a Voxer message (a walkie talkie app that allows my clients to have direct access to me in between our weekly coaching sessions and in times of trouble) from her. *"I'm struggling, "I've got tons of extra work to do and I just feel spread too thin. Thanks to you I recognized that. I usually make my husband's lunch for the next day. Tonight though, I told him he needed to* make it himself. I said it really nice. He didn't even care. Instead, he just said "What do you mean you can't make my lunch? "It'll only take you a few minutes."

I stood my ground and told him I really needed him to do it. But then he said "Fine, I guess I won't be eating lunch tomorrow then." I told him that was pretty sad. He was seriously throwing such a tantrum. It was like I was dealing with my two-year old. What do I do? I don't want him not to eat. Should I just make it? Did I do the right thing?"

"Of course you did the right thing!" I explained. And how I know that is because you knew what you needed, you owned it, and then you **asked** for it. There was something deep inside you that knew you were already stretched too thin. And you honored that. But just because you honored it, doesn't mean that the people around you are going to honor it too; at least not at first anyway. Your husband is a big boy, and if he decides to starve himself the next day, then that is on him, not you. You have officially **rocked the boat**. Welcome aboard my friend."

"I continued, was this the very first time you asked him to make his own lunch?"

"Yeah" she replied.

"Ok, I know you're frustrated with him, but you can't expect your husband to adjust to this new you over night. Cut the man some slack; give him some time to adjust. Keep standing up for your needs, wants and wishes in a gentle, loving way. Communicate more with him. Be vulnerable and *understanding. Try to see things from his perspective rather than making him wrong for not supporting you. This is new territory for him too. He's used to you doing everything so it feels uncomfortable for him. You've trained him to expect these things, and that's ok. Part of this new journey is you <u>un-training</u> him, and that takes time. Have compassion, but that also doesn't mean you start operating from a place of guilt either. That means you allow things to get messy for a bit, you hold your loving ground, and know that eventually things will settle and both of you will find your new norm again."*

The "rocking the boat" phase isn't always fun. In fact, it downright sucks sometimes. Things will get easier and the people in your life will either get on board, or they won't. How will you know either way though if you don't give them a chance?

Designing a lifestyle you want to live is paramount to your happiness. You get one life to live, don't let comfort stand in the way of your happiness.

Ask yourself these few questions:

- In the area of my health what do I most want?

- In the area of my relationships, what do I most want?

- In the area of my career, what do I most want?

- In the area of my finances, what do I most want?

When you're asking these questions, don't let the logistics and the "how's" get in the way. For now, just allow your heart to speak to you.

<u>Now What?</u>

For the last several years whenever I've reached a crossroad, or I'm struggling to make a decision or make a change of some sort, I ask myself two questions.

1. Will I regret *doing* this?

2. Will I regret *not* doing this?

These two questions quickly bring to the surface what's really inside my heart.

Sometimes I even kick it up one more notch. I know this sounds morbid, but I imagine myself lying on my death bed. Thinking about death definitely moves you into a different head space.

If my answer is that I'll regret *not* doing it. I don't waste any time working towards it.

I believe the greatest tragedies aren't the things a person *did* in their life that they regretted, but the things they *didn't* do; the things they left undone. The late Wayne Dyer said it this way: "Don't die with your music still in you." One of my biggest fears is to be on my death bed knowing I didn't reach my fullest potential and knowing I let my fears stand in my way.

When it comes to designing and/or redesigning your life so it's more conducive to your inner most desires be willing to ask yourself those two questions.

If your answer is that you'll regret not doing something, take action and work towards those things. Step outside your comfort zone and rock the boat a little. Chances are, you'll be happy you did.

Pillar 4: F is for Fun

"Happiness is not something ready-made. It comes from your own actions." ~Dalai Lama

This pillar is a must for the busy mom. Moms are known to take life a little too seriously and often be all work and little or no play.

When it comes to describing our daily lives as a mom the word "fun" isn't usually the first that comes to mind.

Screaming kids, wiping poopy butts, cleaning mashed sweet potatoes off the wall, hauling kids from gymnastics to soccer practice, dealing with teenage attitudes, homework, and the endless bedtime routines doesn't always add up to fun and enjoyment.

When I look at the ways I had fun before life with kids, it consisted of getting ready to go out at eight o'clock so we could get to our first stop by ten or eleven. I'd walk out the door in my little black dress that went above my knees and my sexy heels. I'd dance until the wee hours of the morning and end my night at Perkins eating pancakes and bacon. I'd eventually roll out of bed the next day only to lie around watching TV.

Today, as a mom my night ends at the same time my night started in my younger years. By eight o'clock I'm already in my cozy p.j.'s and have my face washed. By ten, I'm almost asleep. Heels? Psshh, the only time I wear those things is when we go to some fancy event or special dinner. And dancing? The last time I danced was when my girlfriend came into town over a year ago, and we were home by 11:00 p.m. Waking up late, I wish. My body is now programmed to wake up at 5:00 a.m., even on the weekends.

Would I change any of this? Heck no. What makes motherhood fun is seeing my kids smile. No matter how old they get I enjoy seeing them happy. It doesn't matter if we're watching a funny movie, camping, or driving to the grocery store, I love seeing my kids smiling. So I often aim for that.

This isn't to say that I don't crave my own forms of fun though.

I most certainly do!

There have been plenty of times that I've dreamt about watching a girly movie of my choice with zero interruptions and meeting friends for dinner. The idea of having drinks without having to wake up early with the kids the next morning, or spontaneously going to lunch with my girlfriends and not worrying about watching the clock for school pickup felt so far away.

Throughout my mom journey I've come to terms

that those moments are but blips in time, a season in my life that won't last forever.

I used to sit around and just wait for each season to pass, but throughout my self-care journey I've realized that I can't afford to put off my own fun anymore. Instead, I've added my own forms of fun without my kids into my life.

Why? Because I *have* to! It makes me sane. It makes me feel like *me* because before I was "mom", I was Jody and that part of me should never be forgotten.

Don't get me wrong, between the endless loads of laundry, planning family activities, running a business, and the infinite number of adult responsibilities; it's easy to forget to have my fun. I've experienced plenty of fun deficits throughout motherhood!

As moms, we have *tons* of really great excuses for this shortage of fun, but the top three are:

- I'm consumed with a busy home life and responsibilities.

- I'm overwhelmed with caring for the family and household.

- We have no extra money to spend on fun activities. (And if we did, I would want to spend it on fun kid stuff.)

The more I refuse to listen to my excuses and find ways to incorporate more fun into my life, the happier I am.

And let's face it, the happier *mama* is, the happier **everyone** is.

Like everything else in this book, finding your own ways to have fun doesn't have to be complicated either. There's plenty of ways around those three excuses I mentioned. Short on cash? Google *"Free events in {insert your city name here}"* or *"Free fun things to do in {insert your city name here}"*. You may have lived in your city for all your life so start viewing it with a fresh set of eyes. Pretend you're someone who's vacationing in your city. It's easy to take for granted and lose sight of what our cities have to offer. If you're open to exploring, you may find yourself surprised at how many cool things you come across.

If you were once the life of the party and now you're the serious, structured, punctual mom, be willing to bring back that playful fun person you once were. Jump in the pool with all your clothes on! Do you have ANY idea how funny and cool your kids would think you were? Crank up the music and dance like a fool in the living room! Those are both *free*.

What is that *something* that gives you life?

Doing fun things that give you joy is a huge piece of this self-care puzzle.

What can you do to find personal joy?

By the way, joy isn't the same as fun but they go together like chips and dip. You can spend the day having an awesome time at the beach but when you get home, you don't have that feeling of joy because your mind was somewhere else.

Or you can have a full body massage and then go to dinner with your husband but somehow a void still lingers. As the day comes to a close and you finally lay your head on your pillow joyfulness might still elude you.

True inner joy, the *"I-feel-good-about-my-life"* emotions takes effort. It requires creating a positive inner core.

Experiencing the fullness of life and opening our eyes to see the radiant colors of a sunrise, appreciating the scent of a home cooked meal, or sharing an intimate chat with a loved one, we become more aware of our daily opportunities for joy. As we cultivate mindfulness, we get more out of life and enjoy more. Finding fun things you desire and doing them <u>mindfully</u> is the gateway to joy.

As busy moms, we don't think in "joy" or "fun", we think in endless tasks and structured schedules.

Fun and personal enjoyment is usually the furthest thing from our minds because we're hyper-focused on bringing those things to our kids and family.

In order to bring more joy to your kids and family, you have to start thinking about yourself. Have some fun and be willing to do more things that give **you** joy. It's not selfish to want these things; it's an act of self-love.

Incorporating more fun helps to balance your emotions, and allows you to receive the emotional support you need to withstand all of the motherly demands that are put on your plate daily.

Maybe you're sitting there saying *"But Jody, my kids bring me so much joy."* Or *"My husband brings me joy."*

I'm sure both are true statements.

However, those two things are dependent on outer circumstances.

What if they were taken away from you? {I know this is extreme and scary to think about and God-willing that will NEVER happen.}

But imagine if it did. What would you be left with then?

Aside from the morbid analogy, hopefully you get my point.

When you leave joy in the hands of others, you

could be setting yourself up for lack of fulfillment and disappointment. Plus, that's also too much to bear on your loved ones. They shouldn't be responsible for providing you all (or most) of your joy.

Looking to our spouses and partners for fun and enjoyment is a bad habit we've all slipped into at one time or another, but it's not a healthy one. Especially if there's not a good balance.

It's easy to look to them for plans and entertainment but it can be just as fun (or even more fun) to do fun things by yourself every now and then. I adore my husband and kids. I thoroughly enjoy spending time with them, especially on the weekends. But--- there are some Saturday's that I just go off on my own.

These days and as I birth this book you're now reading, one of my favorite forms of fun outside the family entails me going to a coffee shop to get some quiet writing time in. When I'm done, I love roaming the streets of the downtown shopping area. They have so many cute shops. I enjoy looking in windows and aimlessly perusing through stores. I thoroughly enjoy chatting with the owners about what inspired them to start their businesses. When I'm done roaming, sometimes I'll go eat lunch by myself. I love sitting at the bar and talking it up with the bartender. To me, hearing other people's stories, learning about their interests and ways of living is so stimulating.

I enjoy doing these things, and I can't do them with my kids or husband in tow. Well, I technically could, but it would be far less enjoyable. My husband calls me "The Mayor" because I'm always trying to chat with strangers. He appeases me most of the time, but sometimes he's like *"C'mon let's keep it moving."*

I <u>need</u> those times to freely be me every once in a while.

Just because I have kids doesn't mean every single weekend has to be devoted to entertaining *them*. I did that for so many years and in the long-run it sucked the life out of me. I have no doubt that it was another contributor to my near burnout in 2010. This new way of doing things has done wonders to my psyche, my parenting, my marriage, and even my health.

Joy has to come from within.

Start leaning into this idea that you don't need anything outside of yourself to receive true joy. It's important you find ways to connect with your *inner* joy. Let your inner child come out and play every once in a while.

This is not to say your family can't provide you with joy, it just means the joy you get from them will be a <u>bonus</u>. It's bonus joy!

The other day, after returning from a nice mini-vacation with my girlfriends, I was getting slammed with life from all sides. My coaching clients had needs, I had deadlines to meet, my son had to be picked up from school early which led to an unexpected emergency room visit and subsequent doctor's appointments, I was starting a writing course and I was diving into a new business venture. Those things were on *top* of everything else I already had going during the work week.

By Wednesday, I had no idea what day it was.

To say I hit the ground running was an understatement.

I have a morning routine that, when *followed*, sets my day up for a good day.

The things in my routine give me daily joy. Waking up and blowing off that routine would have been so easy for me to do this past week.

In fact, I thought about it several times.

I had this inner battle with myself. *"I don't have time to meditate, to read, to journal. I don't have time to write."*

My circumstances were screaming at me.

I knew I didn't have time NOT to do these things though.

Ultimately, all I was really craving was inner

peace and the strength to get through my crazy week.

Peace to know that my day wouldn't be so chaotic. Peace to know that I wouldn't fail as a mom or wife. Peace to know that my clients would be happy and I would meet my deadlines with ease and grace.

Peace to know that when I laid my head on the pillow to go to bed each night, I would feel satisfied and know that I did the best I could.

I also knew the only way for me to acquire the peace I was after, was to start off my morning doing things that brought me joy — even if that meant I had to get up two hours earlier than everybody else.

It was worth it to me.

This meant, even though I was uncomfortable I made the time to meditate, to write, and do things that brought me joy.

If you're at a point in your life where you're unsure of what brings you joy, ask yourself this question *"What did I used to do as a kid to have fun?"* As silly as this might sound, find your answer and then go do it. Yep. I don't care if you liked to build Lego houses. Go do that. Or maybe you loved getting on your bike and going for bike rides. Don't have a bike? Go buy a cheap used one from a thrift store. What is that something you could do for hours as a kid or adult before you had kids?

There's only ever one thing that gets in the way of having fun and that's your <u>beliefs</u>.

Who cares if you feel silly. Let go of the ideas that "you're too old" and "you don't have time" too. Be ruthless about pursuing fun and enjoyment.

At the end of the day, isn't that what you want for your kids too? Fast forward and imagine your kids with a family of their own. Now imagine them being very serious, like robots and never doing anything fun for themselves. I have no doubt in my mind that you would probably pull them aside and say something like *"When was the last time you went fishing with your buddies, you used to love fishing as a kid and even in college."* Or, *"Sweetie, when was the last time you saw your girlfriends? Or painted anything? You were always down in the basement painting when you were little. What happened?"*

Be the example for your kids that you are <u>never</u> too old to have fun. Giving up the fun factor just because you have a family is a death sentence to your soul, and possibly to your marriage too. This isn't just about the *fun*; it's about allowing yourself to be *who* you are. Fun is just another form of self-expression. And in a world filled with distractions and endless demands, you **need** more fun.

I've had a few guy coaching clients over the years and I've heard from many of them *"My wife used to be so much fun before we had kids and now it's like I don't even* know who she is anymore. I feel like I've just been pushed to the side. It takes everything just to get her to go on a date with me anymore. Sometimes I feel like we're just roommates."

Guys need to have fun, and they need us to have fun too.

When my husband and I first started dating, he told me when he got older that he wanted a motorcycle.

I laughed and told him *"No way Jose!"* I loved him too much and if we were still together, there was no way he would get one. The further along we got into our relationship, the more right I felt I had to say it. A couple of years ago while chatting; my husband mentioned "the motorcycle thing" again. (That was my term for it every time he brought it up.) I'd dismissively say *"Are you **still** talking about that "motorcycle thing again"?*

Only this time, I replied *"Yeah, you should get one."* He looked at me like I had just grown a unicorn horn from my forehead. I said *"What? Seriously, you should."* I didn't tell him at the time, but I realized several months back that I had no right to tell him he couldn't get a motorcycle. Who was I to tell him whether or not he could get a bike? Wife or no wife, it wasn't fair for me try to keep him from doing things he enjoyed just because I was fearful of what *could* happen.

I think for anyone to live in the fear of the unknowns is a great tragedy. My husband deserves to enjoy life and do things that are fun to him. If his way of enjoying life is driving a motorcycle, well then I have to put my big girl panties on and deal with it. I need to handle my own shit because at the end of the day, I don't want to rob him of that joy any more than I would want him to rob me of doing the things I enjoy either. It goes both ways.

Back to you now though -- if you want to be a good mom, allow yourself to have more fun. Give yourself the same gift of fun you bring to your kids and be the example that life and parenting can be fun. It's easy to get caught up in life and forget about fun. In the short term it might appear that bypassing fun in order to serve your kids is you being a good mom. However, losing yourself to your kids isn't worth it in the long run. Being a mom and a partner to the person beside you can be exhausting, it takes so much out of us. Fun is like the gas that keeps the car going though.

You need fun.

You **deserve** fun.

Here's a whole list of things you can do to have fun. Pay attention to the things that jump out and jot them down in a notebook so you can refer back to them later. Then go do them.

- The Beach

- Hang with animals

- Fireplaces (with the fire in it of course) and the smell

- Eat chocolate

- Stare up at the clouds

- The smell of vanilla perfume and body wash

- Wearing make up

- Shopping

- Helping people

- Giving compliments

- Rock climbing

- Zip lining

- Sleeping

- Baking sweets

- Soaking up the warm weather

- Binge watching your favorite TV show

- Palm trees

- Sunsets and sunrises

- Ballroom dancing

- Vacations

- Writing

- Reading a good book that you can't put down

- Manicures and pedicures

- Roaming around in nature

- Reminiscing on happy memories

- Talking to an old friend you haven't spoken to in years

- Disney World

- Star gazing on the beach

- Looking at old photos

- Broadway shows

- Sharing or reading words of encouragement

- The view from the top of a mountain

- Sound of ocean waves

- Random daytime sex with your husband/partner

- Chilling in a hammock

- Lying by the pool

- Enjoying a good cup of tea

- Being spontaneous

- Dancing like a fool in the living room

- The smell after it rains

- Back massages

- Lip-syncing in the car to your favorite tunes

- Candle lit dinners

- Making someone laugh or brightening up their day

- Watching a stand-up comedian live, TV, or YouTube

- Hot bubble bath with rose petals and relaxing music

- _____Other

- _____Other

Now What??

1. Pick one or two ways to have fun at *least* once a week.

2. Commit to them, and don't make it complicated.

Developing a Self-Care Practice

Now for the real fun. Let's get down to the nitty gritty of how you can do self-care on the daily.

To make self-care a daily practice, all you have to do is remember this: *Everyday, do one thing to be good to yourself.*

There are two basic types of self-care practices.

The first is *maintenance*.

Maintenance is about creating a day-to-day self-care plan and pinpointing what your daily needs are that will help to keep you (mostly) sane.

The second is what I call "Self-Care 911". This plan is about identifying your needs when faced with a crisis.

Both of these will require a different set of tools.

Neither of these plans are a "one-size-fits-all".

There is however, one common theme to all self-care plans...

Both maintaining and self-care 911 plans are about making a commitment to attend to *all* domains of your life.

These include...

- – Physical health

- – Psychological health

- – Emotional needs

- – Spiritual needs

- – Relationships

In this chapter, we'll go over the steps to create a basic maintenance self-care plan.

Step 1: How Do You Cope Now?

Figuring out what your <u>current</u> self-care habits are, is a big first step in creating a future self-care plan.

How do you usually deal with life's demands? Do you know when it's time to take a break?

When life throws you a challenge or two, are you more likely to lean towards using a positive coping strategy or negative one?

The following are some examples of each. Check mark which ones you use...

<u>Negative Coping Skills</u>

__ Biting your nails

___ Mindlessly eating

___ Drinking excessive alcohol

___ Using drugs

___ Skipping meals

___ Pacing

___ Yelling

___ Driving erratically

___ Smoking

___ Withdrawing from family and friends

___ Other

___ Other

_____

_____

Positive

___ Taking a hot bubble bath

___ Reading

___ Chatting with a friend

___ Socializing with a friend(s)

__ Taking deep breaths

__ Meditating

__ Engaging in a hobby you enjoy

__ Listening to music

__ Going for a walk

__ Stretching

__ Exercising

__ Being in nature

__ Other

__ Other

_____

_____

Take an honest look at your *current* behaviors. If you find that you're more often reaching for a glass of wine, drugs, or lashing out at loved ones instead of giving yourself a mommy time out during times of overwhelm and struggle, it may be time to reassess your go-to coping skills.

Step 2: Pinpoint Your Self-Care Needs

Everyone is faced with challenges and everyone's self-care needs are different.

In this section, let's take a second to consider what your *everyday* self-care needs are.

These are the things you need on a <u>daily</u> basis in order to maintain your sanity --Errr...I mean self-care.

Remember that self-care goes well beyond your basic *physical* needs i.e. eating, exercising, sleeping, brushing your teeth, showering.

A true self-care plan considers you as <u>whole</u>; your physical, emotional, psychological, social, financial, spiritual, career, and financial well-being.

On a day-to-day basis, what are you doing to support your overall well-being? Do you currently practice self-care in your day? Do you excel in some areas of self-care more than others?

Maybe your "current self-care" plan is nonexistent...that's ok too.

This is a great place to start.

Ok, let's get to it! Use the area below to help you identify which areas you might need extra support.

1.) **Emotional**: i.e. Doing positive activities, expressing how you feel in a healthy productive way, acknowledging your own accomplishments, engaging in positive self-talk, etc.

Current Practices:

_____

_____

_____

Practices to Try:

_____

_____

_____

2.) **Spiritual/Religious**: i.e. Spending time praying, spending time in nature, meditating, sitting quietly self-reflecting, reading something uplifting or inspirational, attending a spiritual or religious service, attending a workshop or group session, etc.

Current Practices:

_____

_____

_____

Practices to Try:

_____

_____

_____

3.) **Physical**: i.e. moving your body daily, eating healthy meals regularly, good sleeping habits, regular exercise, staying current on regular medical and/or holistic check-ups, etc.

Current Practices:

_____

_____

_____

Practices to Try:

_____

_____

_____

4.) **Financial**: i.e. Creating a budget or other financial plan, paying off debts, awareness of how finances impacts the quality of your life, positive self-talk/affirmations around money, etc.

Current Practices:

_____

_____

_____

Practices to Try:

_____

_____

_____

5.) **Professional**: i.e. maintaining work-life balance, maintaining mommy-life balance, having positive work relationships, good time management skills, pursuing work that is meaningful to you, etc.

Current Practices:

_____

_____

_____

Practices to Try:

_____

_____

_____

6.) **Psychological**: i.e. journaling, hiring a life coach, taking time out for yourself, pursuing hobbies or new interests, taking a break from electronic devices, etc.

Current Practices:

_____

_____

_____

Practices to Try:

_____

_____

_____

7.) **Social**: i.e. Making time for your family and friends, carving out time to go on dates with your spouse/partner, maintaining healthy relationships, releasing toxic relationships, asking for support from your friends and family if needed, etc.

Current Practices:

_____

_____

_____

Practices to Try:

_____

_____

_____

The amount of *time* you spend on any of the above things isn't nearly as important as you *doing* them <u>daily</u>. It doesn't need to be a long drawn out process (unless you want it to be). Don't over-complicate this. It can be as little as two minutes, as long as an entire day, or anywhere in between. The point is to intentionally spend time doing something for **you**, every single day.

For years, I always sat down on Sunday nights and looked at the week ahead on my calendar to see what I had going on. If I had business meetings, doctor's appointments or a school function I'd just start plugging in my daily self-care around my appointments. I'd take whatever was leftover in my schedule. If I had three business meetings and a school event to attend at my son's school, I wouldn't get anything that day because there just wasn't enough time.

It took me a few years to finally realize I was doing it all backwards. Yes, I was making time for myself when I could but I wasn't making it a top priority. I was allowing my schedule to dictate when I practiced my self-care when it should be the other way around. So I began reversing my calendar. I started plugging in my self-care a few weeks to a month ahead so that whatever business meetings or doctor's appointments I had would be planned _around_ my self-care.

I knew I had to do it this way or I'd never tend to myself. I didn't want my business, household, or family needs to take over my schedule. I wanted to put myself first and I wanted that to show up in my calendar.

It's really done wonders for not letting my daily self-care practice get pushed to the side.

The basic principle is to make sure self-care gets into your calendar. The calendar symbolizes importance, and your self-care practice is the single _most_ important thing in your life. I know that's a radical idea, but sit with it for a minute. Everything else should come _after_ your self-care. Adding it into your calendar solidifies it, and you'll be less likely to forget about yourself.

I get asked a lot, "What do you do for self-care every day?" So I'll walk you through a day in the life of Jody. Keep in mind though, I've been practicing for years and I no longer have young kids. My oldest is twenty and he works full-time so I don't really "take care of him" anymore; at least not physically anyway.

I'm also a coach and this is my career. Similar to that of a fitness coach, I live and breathe self-care. For me, it's a lifestyle. This also doesn't mean I do it perfectly every single day either. More often than not I do it, but never perfectly.

Don't let my plan intimidate you, just tweak to fit your own lifestyle. Remember, do not make this complicated, the important thing is to simply do small things every day to fill up your cup in ways that are meaningful to you.

The below is a sample schedule for during the school year. My self-care practices are in **bold**.

5:30am- **Stretch, read, write in my gratitude journal and if I'm writing a book, I write.**

7a.m. **Walk, ride my bike, or do another form of exercise**

8.a.m Make sure my (middle school) son is up getting ready for school and doing his morning chores. **Shower and while I'm in there I have my phone sitting on the towel rack with some form of inspiration or other spiritual audio playing; either a podcast, an audio book, a YouTube video, or meditation music.**

9 a.m. **I mindfully eat a healthy breakfast that will fuel my body. By mindfully, I mean I eat slowly and enjoy each bite while keeping my mind in the present moment and not the next thing on my schedule or that I need to do. The bowl or plate I use is one I picked out special for me, it brings a smile to my face every time I use it (and my kids aren't allowed to touch them). I take my handful of vitamins.** Clean up the kitchen.

9:30: **Meditate. Sometimes I use a guided meditation on an app called Insight Timer. Other times I listen to soft music. Every so often I just sit without anything.**

10:00 a.m. Coaching calls, writing, or other work stuff.

12 p.m. **I mindfully eat my lunch (using my special bowl or plate).** Once finished, while **I'm brushing my teeth I repeat the affirmations taped on my bathroom mirror. Then I take my mid-day vitamins.**

12:30 p.m. **Meditate**.

12:45 p.m. Prep for any afternoon coaching calls.

{**Note** Even though I work from home, I still gave myself a lunch break just like I would if I still had an office job. This helps to prevent the afternoon slump.}

1:00 p.m. Coaching calls, writing, or other work stuff.

3:15 p.m. Wrap up my work day. **Sit on my bed and take a few deep breaths or do a five-minute** meditation so I can get ready to leave my work day behind me and put on my mom hat.

3:30 p.m. Leave to pick up my son from school. On the way there **I'm listening to an inspirational or educational audio. I.e. podcast, YouTube, etc. Or, I'm chatting with a friend to get some laughs in.**

4:45 p.m. Arrive home. I go upstairs to **change into my comfy clothes and wash off my makeup. If I didn't have any on, I still wash it so I feel refreshed and ready to handle the night routine.** As I'm washing my face, **I'm reading the affirmations on my mirror.** If it's my night to cook, I head downstairs to start dinner. If it's not, I jump back on my computer and wrap up my work day while my son is doing his own forms of self-care and decompressing from his school day.

6:00 p.m. **Mindfully eat dinner.** Clean up the kitchen, get son going on his homework and nighttime chores.

7:30 p.m. **Family time.**

8:30 p.m. Quiet time for everyone. **I usually read, journal, meditate, write down 3 things I was grateful for that day, or take a hot bath. Sometimes I do all of them, most of the time I do one or two.**

10 p.m. Make sure my son's lights are out and say goodnight to both my kids. **Before I drift off to sleep I set my intentions for the next day. I pretend I have a**

magic wand and I envision exactly how I want the day to go. I call this "pre-paving".

Now What?

1.) Plug self-care into your calendar. Do what feels comfortable to you. If planning your self-care for the entire month feels overwhelming right now, then start with just a week or two ahead. You don't have to block out hours in your calendar. Start with fifteen minutes a few times a week to get you going. As your comfort levels increase, work towards doing more every single day.

Self-Care 911

When it comes to creating your 911 plan you want to prepare and develop it the same way you would for any other emergency situations.

Ahead of time.

It's vital you figure out what your plan is <u>prior</u> to actually needing to implement the 911-plan.

This way, you have the time and the head space to think effectively.

So, if you're not currently facing a crisis, continue reading this chapter anyway. Now is the perfect time.

There's self-care, and then there's SELF-CARE.

Your normal everyday self-care plan will look entirely different than your self-care 911 plan.

Self-Care 911 is for the seasons or times in your life where shit is hitting the fan way more than normal.

It could be a death in the family, a flood, the flu, a crumbling marriage, a divorce, an ill elderly parent, a move, a career change, a loss of job, a health scare, a bankruptcy, an extended period of caregiving to a parent, a fire, a child diagnosed with a serious illness or disease.

Or, a hurricane.

I live in Florida so hurricanes are fairly common in the months of August and September.

This past hurricane season was no different.

If you weren't living in a bubble, I'm sure you heard about the monster of a hurricane by the name of *Irma*. Its projected path was to be a direct hit to the Tampa Bay area – where we lived – and, as a category *five*. The largest of them all.

The entire state of Florida was under a "*State of Emergency*". Our city issued evacuation orders and in our zone it was *mandatory* we leave.

Self-Care 911 was officially activated.

The days leading up to the evacuation though were an emotional roller coaster as we watched the storm come closer and closer.

Hotels in neighboring Georgia, gas for our cars, and gallons of water jugs became limited. Canned goods were flying off the grocery store shelves at lightning speed. People on the roads were driving like crazed lunatics; people were shoving others in stores fighting over gas cans.

Florida was in total panic mode.

We were lucky to have nabbed two hotel rooms for four nights in Georgia when we did because the next day the evacuation order was issued, and there were none to be had. Actually, we weren't *"lucky"*. That was me listening to my intuitive guidance/gut. Because of my self-care plan, my mind was quiet enough to be able to hear the "nudges" I felt, and later honor them. It's hard to do that if our minds are racing with fear. My husband thought I was overreacting *"because the hurricane hadn't even reached a category 3 yet"*. But guess who was glad I booked it. Yep, the hubs.

Ok, moving on.

My head had a zillion thoughts at first though. I found myself literally spinning in circles. I'd aimlessly walk from room to room thinking about what I needed to grab for our impromptu road trip.

We had no idea what we would come back to. It could be a direct hit, which would involve heavy winds, rain, and tornadoes. Or, we could get the storm surge and possibly come back to a completely flooded house.

Our family car is a Toyota Prius. In it, we had to fit myself, my husband, one very tall nineteen-year-old son, and my twelve-year-old son.

Oh, and two dogs.

Plus, our clothes and whatever things from the house we wanted to save.

I had no clue where to begin.

There was so much to do I couldn't even think straight.

I went from my living room to the kitchen, to the storage room...and I wasn't accomplishing anything really. My thoughts were all over the place.

That's usually a very clear indicator that I'm spending way too much time in my head and not enough time mindfully centered and connected to my heart.

My head was foggy and I was paralyzed with indecision.

My mind raced, *"I need to grab the important papers from the filing cabinet; I have to get my family out of here! I still need to grab that load of laundry out of the dryer; I can't forget to bring the dog food, oh and poop bags. We need poop bags, I wonder if Josh grabbed D batteries yet? Did the heavy duty flashlight get delivered yet...?"*

There were so many needs that I couldn't even keep up with myself.

In an attempt to get my act together I went into the bathroom and threw some water on my face.

"Alright Jody get it together. Stop freaking out and get a grip."

I stood at the sink and suddenly remembered that nothing was more important than up-leveling my self-care practice right now. If I really wanted this to go as smooth as possible I had to do whatever it took to calm my crazed lunatic inner chatter.

My poor attempt to get things done came to a screeching halt.

I stopped and did the unthinkable.

While everyone in our neighborhood was putting up their hurricane shutters and bolting plywood to their windows, I jumped on my bike.

You know, the kind you actually pedal.

My logical brain told me this was the exact *opposite* of what I needed to do. My heart on the other hand, told me this was *exactly* what I needed to do.

For me, meditating is a big part of my daily self-care plan. I *love* sitting and just allowing my mind to quiet. That wasn't an option though, not this time.

I knew I wouldn't be able to sit still. I felt anxious and I knew my thoughts wouldn't slow down. In order for me to move through the energy of what I was feeling, I had to move my body <u>physically</u>. I *intuitively* knew that.

Thinking clearly was an absolute must and I knew if I truly wanted to serve my family the best I could, I needed to give myself time to just **be**.

I pedaled my ass all around my favorite lake and through the streets of the downtown area.

I waved and smiled at everyone rushing to put their shutters and plywood up.

They looked at me like I had lost my mind.

I smiled anyway.

When I first started to pedal, my mind was still rattling off the million things still needing to get done. I was still on the verge of tears and I still felt *overwhelmed*.

All it took were just a few short moments and the wind hitting my face before I noticed my mind starting to settle.

My thoughts were no longer racing with fear, doubt and worry.

I felt like I could breathe again.

My shoulders relaxed.

I felt alive.

For this brief moment of time, I left *everything* behind.

I felt calm and clear-headed.

I felt in my heart that everything was going to be ok.

The panic began to subside.

The anxiety lifted and I could physically feel my entire body relaxing.

When I returned home a half-hour later, I was able to take action with ease. I calmly communicated to my family exactly what I needed help with. Our trip really couldn't have gone any better. We got everything we needed to get done and we safely arrived in Georgia right on time. Even with traffic and numerous gas stations closed because they had zero gas to sell, we made it a fun adventure rather than a stressful nightmare. In fact, when I look back on it today, it's with nostalgia. Thankfully, we had a home to return to also.

The rule of thumb to live by is when shit really hits the fan in life; it's time to up-level your self-care practice.

Life with kids and family is already chaotic in itself.

When we add circumstances that aren't usually there, it puts an extra strain on *everything*.

It doesn't matter if it's a beautiful birth of a new

baby, caring for a sick child, or moving – things can get nuts!

Last year, my twelve-year-old son needed more than usual healthcare. All of a sudden he started getting these super bad headaches and a lot of dizziness.

They got so bad that I'd have to pick him up from school, a lot.

I'm usually the mom who under-reacts to these things. I guess I've been a mom long enough to not really freak out because I've seen so many things with both my boys. Broken arms, busted lips, stitches, appendix that burst, pneumonia – they've all helped to desensitize me a bit. Plus, when you're the daughter of a nurse, you grow up hearing *"You're fine. Just go sit on the toilet."*

So naturally I've been programmed to share the same wisdom with my own kids; unless a body part is broken, falling off, you're bleeding, you have a raging fever, or you're puking, *"you're fine."*

His headaches though, they freaked me out. They came on suddenly and paralyzed him with pain. It was awful to witness.

When I took him in to see his pediatrician, she seemed a tad alarmed too.

We both knew this was out of character for my

otherwise healthy son. I felt like she was deliberately trying to act as though she wasn't too concerned. I could tell she knew something wasn't right though. My mommy intuition knew it too. His doctor said *"Let's get him in to get an MRI of his brain and see what's going on."*

Her confirmation that this needed to be addressed simultaneously made me feel better and it freaked me out even more.

We saw her on a Wednesday. She got the MRI scheduled for the next morning and now we were waiting for the results. She told me she would call me by Friday and warned me that it might even be after hours, but no matter the time she would call me with the results before the weekend. It was now Friday night and I had just dropped my son to spend the weekend with his dad.

As I drove over the bay bridge on my way home, I felt compelled to pull off and watch the beautiful sunset. I needed to *breathe*. I wanted nothing more than to regain my balance and decompress from the crazy week before I headed back home. I knew his doctor was going to call eventually with the results, and her timing couldn't have been better.

Sitting in my car listening to music and watching the sun drop, the phone rang.

I looked down at the caller ID *"John Hopkins All Children's Hospital"*.

My heart sunk and started to beat fast.

"Hello, this is Jody?"

"Hi Jody. Sorry to call you so late, I just received the results back from the MRI. Ok. So the MRI shows that Evan has something pressing on the back of his brain where it meets his spine. We don't think it's a tumor; it's likely something called Chiari Malformation. That's something he would've been born with and it basically means that the brain tissue extends into the spinal canal. Essentially, his brain is too big for his skull. Chiari malformation isn't life threatening, but we do need to do another MRI this time with contrast and then a test to measure the flow of his spinal fluid. If that appears to be diminished or slow, he may need to have what's called a decompression surgery of his brain.

But let's just take one step at a time; I've already spoken with the Neurosurgeon. Let's get you scheduled with him so he can better assess the necessity for surgery or not. His office is expecting your call so you can call anytime on Monday to schedule that appointment. We'll get those tests ordered in the meantime."

We chatted for a few more minutes and then I hung up the phone.

My head was spinning as I swirled her words around in my head.

"Don't think it's a tumor? Brain surgery? Chiari?

Born with it? She already spoke to the brain surgeon? Malformation? What?"

I lost it.

I sat there watching the sun go down bawling.

The ugly kind.

I just let it out. It was too much to take in.

Eventually, I gathered myself together as much as I possibly could so I could call my mom. She was anxiously waiting for the results too. So was my son's dad and my husband, but first things first. I needed my mom.

All it took was for her to say *"Hello?"* and I lost it again.

Now we were both ugly crying.

It was quite the scene.

The initial weeks of his diagnosis were a complete emotional roller coaster, and *nutty* to say the least.

Thankfully, his spinal flow test came back normal and he didn't end up needing the surgery.

He's just followed closely by his team of doctors.

During the process of jumping from doctor to doctor and completing the required testing in the hospital, at times I felt like a rag doll.

As if I was being pushed and pulled in this direction and that. As his mom, I felt this pull to devote every ounce of my attention, love, and care for my son in any way possible. He had his own set of concerns and worries and he needed me more than ever; physically, and *emotionally*.

At the same time though – I knew I had to devote that same love, care, and compassion towards myself too. I needed to make sure I stayed grounded for the sake of my son, as well as for myself and the rest of my family.

I knew it was imperative for me to not only <u>maintain</u> my self-care practice, but to kick it up a notch.

That didn't always feel like the "logical" thing, but intuitively I knew it was the *best* thing to do.

If what I wanted more than anything was to give my son and family love, affection, and support, I had to fill my cup up every time I did something to fill theirs.

Otherwise, I wouldn't have much to offer anyone.

It was a tricky line to walk though.

It helped to watch out for certain indicators; such as:

- Feeling scared

- Feeling exhausted

- Feeling overwhelmed

- Feeling burnt-out

- Feeling anxious

- Feeling like I want to run and hide

- Feeling like I needed a silent retreat

These are red flags that force me to ask myself *"What have I done for myself lately?"*

If it's been a while I'll choose to do one or two of the following (<u>regardless</u> of how many other things are on my to-do list):

– Go for a walk

– Take a hot bath

– Write my book or journal

– Read something inspirational

– Sit by the water

– Walk on the beach

– Meditate

– Sit in the sun for fifteen minutes

Doing these things is an <u>investment of my time</u>.

I seriously can't even express this enough.

They don't take away from anything, or anyone – they add value.

Not only does doing these things help make me feel whole and allow me to be fully present, but they make me an even *better* caregiver too.

The more things I have on my plate and the more things that are being thrown at me are the days I slow down.

Not necessarily *physically*, but <u>mentally</u>.

My internal dialog must be reflective of what I want and not a long list of things I don't want, or things I fear, stress or worry about.

It's easy to get caught up in the trap of aimlessly letting my mind wander down a road that will only deplete my energy and bring me down.

The more I quiet my mind, either through meditation or just taking a few deep breaths, the more present and calm I become.

Ok now that we have the basics covered; let's get into the nitty-gritty of what your self-care 911 plan might look like.

Ask for Help:

Now is not super-hero time. Now is the time to lean on friends and family. Now is the time to ask and accept help from others. Now is the time to **take time for yourself and rely** *on the people around you more.*

Your family needs you now more than ever, so it's *imperative* you take care of yourself first and foremost. I know, I know - this feels counterproductive.

Remember though, taking a moment to yourself is an <u>investment</u> of time. In order to serve your family the best way you can, you will need to do what you need to do to take care of and be good to <u>yourself</u>.

In times of crisis or extra stressful times, you basically embark on a self-care boot camp.

I had a coaching client who was helping her grown son with his daughter's first birthday. My client told her son and daughter-in-law they could have it at their house. It was a really big to-do. Less than a week before the party though, the in-laws got sick and they weren't able to do what they initially said they could help with.

My client called me in tears. She was so upset and stressed to the max. Her to-do list was a mile long and she had been up all night decorating and trying to get the house ready as much as she could in advance. The party was in three days and there was a lot to be done.

With little sleep and the added stress, she woke up that morning with a sore throat, a headache, and she felt like a truck ran her over.

My advice?

"Go back to bed and take the day off. Don't touch another thing for this party."

Of course that was the *opposite* of what she felt like she *"should"* do. Logistically she felt as though there was a time shortage since the party was just days away.

I explained to her that her body was screaming for help. She had to honor it; otherwise she might be *really* sick for the party. This was the last thing she or anyone else would want.

When you give yourself the time and space to rest in stressful times and you fully *surrender*, a funny thing happens.

Things miraculously fall into place. Ideas and solutions flow and the right people show up to help in times of need.

That's exactly what happened for my client.

Everything came together perfectly. She had a few of her close friends bring a couple of dishes and she readjusted the menu to a simpler one.

It took a great deal of willpower to accept and receive help, but she had no other choice but to open her arms to receive.

Priorities:

In times of crisis, prioritizing will be key.

Laundry, a clean house, the dishes in the sink…they can wait. They're not important.

Let them go.

Sure, it would be nice to have those things done, and they *will* get done in due time. Now is not the time though.

Ask yourself this question *"What is most important right now?"*

Maybe it's calling a sitter in for a few hours so you can rest, or get some other things done. Maybe it's asking your spouse, parent, or other family member to take over for a couple of hours in the morning while you handle other stuff. Or maybe you just want to sit by the beach and get that body some much needed Vitamin D. Alone. {They don't call it "beach therapy" for nothing.}

<u>You</u> know what's most important to get done. What will get in the way of it though is this false belief that *everything* needs to get done, *right now*, and *all* by you, and you <u>alone</u>.

That's baloney.

You're a human, dealing with a crisis. Now is the time to do what? Yep ---- up-level your self-care practice and chill a little more.

Rest

Here's something to think about; instead of shoving ten cups of coffee down your throat to get through your day, try sleeping when your body is tired.

{GASP!!!!}

Who would have thought!

Sleep when you're tired!?

Noooooo....

YES!!!!

There's nothing wrong with drinking an extra cup of coffee for a day or two to help you get through the initial phase of the crisis, but anything longer than a couple of days is bound to catch up with you.

Instead of caffeine, try honoring the warnings your body is giving you. If you're tired, it's because your body needs *rest*. It's literally crying out for help.

Honor this cry.

Set your timer for 20-30 minutes and close your damn eyes. Allow yourself to completely relax. Everything you need to get done will still be there when you wake up. Let it sit there for now.

The only one putting pressure on you is yourself.

When you wake up and return to these tasks later, your level of effectiveness will increase if you give yourself permission to recharge your batteries and reboot yourself.

Go take a nap. Zzzzzz.

Just Say NO!

Isn't this what we tell our kids?

If you really want to drive yourself mad, just keep saying yes to everything. Keep piling on the duties, the chores, the events, the expectations and all the requests from others.

Ask yourself honestly, *"Am I saying yes to others more than I'm saying yes to myself?"*

Be a "yes snob". Be ultra-picky about the things you say yes to.

If it doesn't <u>feel</u> right, politely decline.

You can't possibly please everybody all the time; especially not in the face of a challenge or crisis. This is about <u>your</u> needs, not "other peoples".

Who cares what people will think if you say no to baking ten sheets of brownies for the bake sale, or not volunteering as a field trip parent or snack mom for your kids' baseball team.

Keep the number of tasks and projects you accept to a low one (or two) a month during these stressful times.

Guilt – Let It Go

The definition of guilt: *The fact of having committed a specified or implied offense or crime.*

"Implied offense." Who's doing the *implying*, because if it's me…I'm in trouble.

I can be my own worst enemy.

By nature, and with good intentions, I tend to be a people pleaser too.

If I'm not careful, I can easily fall into this trap.

I'm so much more aware these days though, so it's easier to catch it and readjust.

Sometimes not only do I try to do it all, but when I can't…I start beating myself up for it.

Which is nuts.

Remember what I said earlier?

Mom guilt will *always* be there. It's not going away anytime soon.

That's the bad news.

The good news is that you can easily decide to kick it out of the driver's seat whenever you'd like.

The more awareness you have and realize just how much you operate on guilt, the sooner you can stop the madness and end the guilt-trips.

If you're going to get through this crazy season in your life, you have to be willing to put yourself *__first__*, now more than ever before.

Yes, you might be taking care of others more than usual, but you will be able to take **better** care of them when you take care of yourself first.

So what if you put yourself in a time out to stare off into space for ten minutes while others are cleaning your house or picking up your kid.

So what if you watch your favorite funny TV shows in the middle of the day.

So what if you let your kid play video games or tell them to go outside just so you can enjoy some peace and quiet to yourself for an hour or two.

So what if you don't feel like cooking and end up ordering take-out...two nights in a row. Or three.

Woopty doo.

Moms. We sure do love to pile on the guilt as if some things are indicators of our parenting skills or how much we love our kids, or family.

The truth of the matter is, our kids are not going to grow up and say, *"Well, there was hope for me...until my mom decided to order take out two nights in a row."*

So, the choice is yours...sanity or guilt? It's up to you.

Do what you need to do to find joy in your life and don't let guilt stop you.

Laugh, Often.

Laughter is the best medicine - for everything. When you feel overwhelmed or catch yourself beating yourself up for not working at the "normal" capacity, just ask yourself *"Does this really matter in the big picture??"*

And then laugh out loud.

Yes ---just start laughing at yourself. In fact, belly laugh at yourself.

At first, you'll feel like an idiot. This causes you to laugh at yourself and then you laugh at yourself for laughing at yourself.

It's contagious and really pretty funny actually.

Or, you could always find funny videos to laugh at...pets and kids are great ones to search on YouTube.

There's tons of scientific evidence that backs up the idea that laughter is literally the best medicine.

Give Yourself Permission to Feel Bad – Schedule It In Your Day

It's OK that you're not feeling your peppy positive self. Give yourself permission to just feel bad. You feel the way that you do for a reason, and it's only for a season.

Let that be OK.

Set a timer for fifteen, or thirty minutes, or even an hour. However long you need.

Here's a quote I came up with a few years back...*"You've got to feel it before you can heal it."*

This holds true for any emotion you might be feeling.

In order to heal it, you must be willing to do what's hard, and allow yourself to feel it.

Give yourself permission to feel the way you do. If it's sadness, grief, anger, worry, fear or disappointment, **feel** it.

Don't try to feel any other way than the way you do right now. Set your timer and just feel it.

You won't feel this way forever and the more you allow yourself to feel your emotions, the quicker you'll heal. If you keep trying to shove your feelings down, they will eventually pop back up. Feel them now so you can heal.

No Major Life Decisions

Now is *not* the time to think about going back to school or going for the across the country move you've been thinking about. Table any thoughts of a divorce or career change too.

This all gets put on hold.

For now.

It's only temporary.

The problem with pursuing major life decisions in a time of crisis is that your judgment is fogged. It's way too much to handle on your already fragile psyche.

If there are too many things thrown at you at once, it could catch up with you and make matters worse in the long run.

If it can be put on the back burner for a bit, do it.

Give yourself permission to just breathe right now. Resume the major life decisions again once things have settled a bit.

Don't worry, you're not missing out. There'll be

plenty of opportunities out there when you and your family are ready. Who knows, there may even be better one by the time you're truly ready.

<u>Exercise – Even Just a Little Bit</u>

You may not be motivated or have any energy to exercise. So don't. Just be willing to move your body. Movement is not only meant for losing weight, it's also a great way to improve your mental state. It's medicine for your body.

When you move your body, you are moving energy. And when you move energy, you move toxins and other things out of your body.

It's a natural way for your body to decompress from stress.

There are tons of case studies proving that exercise is good for the mind as well as the body. Moving your body is an amazing mood booster and can be an effective treatment for anxiety, grief, depression and even insomnia.

If you don't feel like working out, aim to walk one thousand steps a day. That's a mere half-mile.

Increase as much as your little heart desires. The point is to just *move*. If you'd enjoy yoga or riding your bike more, then do that. What you do isn't nearly as important as just finding joyful ways to move your body right now.

Meaningful Practices

Do more of what you love and things you enjoy.

This could include, meditation, prayer, walking in the woods, hiking up a mountain, sowing, sitting quietly, reading inspirational material, taking a bath, binge watching your favorite shows, or writing in your journal.

It doesn't really matter <u>what</u> you do, as long as you <u>enjoy</u> doing it.

In times of crisis, it's easy to push these things off to the side. Throughout this difficult time though, you'll want to make sure you're doing them every day.

The point is to do something you **enjoy** because this will help you decompress from stress or other negative emotions you might be facing. It might not completely take your mind off things, or it might. You'll never know unless you try.

Give it a go and do something you like to do.

Every single day.

Let Yourself Cry

Maybe you're the type to rarely let your emotions get the best of you.

That's great, but now is not the time for that.

Unleash the tears.

Give yourself permission to bawl your eyes out and ugly cry if that's what you feel like doing.

If you're constantly feeling that lump in your throat, but rarely shedding tears, that's an indication you're not letting yourself cry.

Stop that.

Shut yourself in a room and open the flood gates.

It's OK to cry. In fact, it's <u>healthy</u> to cry.

Crying is a necessity if you want to heal and eventually bounce back from this stressful time.

Unless you're a robot or some other form of artificial intelligence, you **need** to cry.

Crying isn't for the weak, it's cleansing to the soul. Let your tears fall where they may.

Don't be ashamed for the way you feel, you're going through a lot right now, crying is a healthy way of coping.

<u>Small Actions</u>

You might feel as if your life is spinning out of control and if you're anything like me, you hate the feeling of that.

Accepting what is, is a <u>huge</u> part of your healing process. You cannot control everything.

However, you <u>can</u> take small actions to help make you feel you're getting your life back.

Do the most important things in the morning since this is likely when you'll have the most energy. (Unless you're a night owl, then do this in reverse.)

Do one thing at a time.

Don't try to tackle everything at once.

Switching from one thing to the next is way less effective and can make you feel scatter brained too.

If you're feeling tired and don't have the energy to push through all your tasks in one day, give yourself X amount of time to complete each task.

For example, let's say you have a list of things that need to get done but you only have four hours.

Within those four hours, work for an hour and then give yourself a fifteen-minute break before working the next hour.

You'll be more efficient rather than pushing through the entire four hours without stopping.

<u>**Ditch the "Shoulds"**</u>

Stop "shoulding" all over yourself.

Common "shouldings" are...

- I should forgive

- I should be compassionate

- I should meditate

- I should be more productive

- I should spend more time with the kids

- I should spend more time with my spouse/partner

- I should feel more awake

- I should be happier

- I should clean the house

- I should exercise more

- I should be more appreciative

- I should lose weight

- I should be grateful to be alive

When you approach each task, ask yourself throughout the day *"Am I doing this because I want/need to do it or because I think I <u>should</u> do it?"* If the reason is because you *"<u>should</u>"* then ask yourself this: *"Why?*

What do I fear will happen if I don't do this?"

Set aside an hour every day as a "should-free" zone -- this is a time when you only attend to things you shamelessly <u>want</u> to do. If a "should" pops up, set it aside for later or let it go completely.

Talk It Out With a Professional

Sometimes a family member or friend just doesn't cut it and its time to bring a professional on board. You may choose to hire a therapist, or a life coach like myself to help you get through this challenging season.

It takes courage to ask for help, and it is a true sign of strength.

Let someone else be your guide for a while. Cut yourself some slack and allow someone else to see things that you may not be seeing right now.

Define "Normal"

It's easy to get caught up in the thought that how you're reacting isn't "normal". Or that you "should" be reacting this way or that.

Everybody handles a crisis differently and you won't know how you or anyone else will handle something until you're put to the test and are actually facing the crisis yourself.

How **you're** handling it is just fine. Be gentle with

yourself. Be kind to yourself and know that you're doing the best you can right now. Sure, you may not be handling this "perfectly", but who's the judge?

Give yourself this space.

You'll learn and grow from any challenge you face.

This is your path right now.

I know as painful as these days might be you're learning so much about yourself.

You're exactly where you ought to be so don't let anyone else tell you differently.

Accept Your Own Shortcomings

You are perfectly imperfect.

We all have areas that we naturally excel in. We also have plenty of things we can work on too.

Don't let your "weaknesses" define you. Instead, focus on your *strengths*.

When we're going through something exceptionally challenging, everything becomes heightened. Our emotions increase and we can often become overly critical of ourselves.

I love social media just as much as the next person, but it can also be the worst breeding ground for comparison.

How often do you mindlessly scroll through updates and then suddenly feel crappy? That's likely because you didn't even notice you were comparing yourself to everyone you saw. *"Ohhhh, she looks so put together." "Look how thin she got!" "I wish my husband would do stuff like that for me." Her house is beautiful; I wish we had a bigger house. Gosh, she always looks so confident..."* It's in this land of comparing you get lost in your weaknesses rather than shining the light on your strengths.

A person who might *appear* to have it "all together" – also has weaknesses. They're there. You just can't see them as easily as you can see your own.

Love yourself while you continue to improve yourself. Allow yourself to be imperfect, especially right now while you're going through this extra challenging time.

Look back on your life and acknowledge everything you've overcome thus far. How many times have you been faced with change and stressful times and you've come out stronger than before? A lot probably.

The best way to get through tough times is to love yourself through it.

Life isn't perfect, it's sometimes messy and not at

all the way you pictured it.

Happiness is a choice though. You can choose to be happy in the messiness of life or you can choose to be miserable.

Both take work and energy. The latter has the potential to suck the life out of you and the first has the potential to GIVE you life, love and peace.... regardless of what's going on around you.

Today, may you choose to be happy in the messiness of your life.

May you rise above your circumstances and see the love, and all the goodness around you.

Be easier on yourself. Cut yourself more slack.

Again, when you're faced with a crisis, you most likely won't have the time (or energy) to create a healthy coping strategy.

It's so much easier to take the time to plan ahead while you're not in a state of major distress.

The area below will help you to pinpoint your own self-care needs when times are extra tough. The more you can engage in healthy habits and avoid the harmful ones during these times, the better off you'll be.

Now is the time to put you and your needs *first*. I

really can't express this enough.

Now What?

In each section, I'll give you some examples of healthy and harmful coping mechanisms. These might be things you're already doing and they're working great for you. However, there might be a few that aren't working for you, so you'll want to replace those with better ones.

Healthy activities will be all the things that promote good feelings, make you feel empowered and uplift you. These are the things that will lift your spirits.

The harmful activities are the things that will do the opposite. They'll drag you down and leave you feeling bad; physically and/or emotionally. These will be the things you'll want to steer away from.

In the space below, your job now is to fill in the blanks. Our goal here is to shed light on the dark parts of yourself so you can begin to incorporate healthier ways to cope.

Self-Talk: Try to think about what you would say to a friend or family member with the same struggles and apply it to yourself.

Healthy self-talk: *"I love and accept myself right now." "I release my fears." "I am safe." "I have the strength I need to get through this." I'm doing better than most."*

"Don't be so hard on yourself."

Harmful self-talk: *"I can't do this." "I knew this would happen to me, I deserve this. I suck."*

Healthy:

_____

_____

_____

_____

_____

Harmful:

_____

_____

_____

_____

_____

Mood: Which activities help to encourage a positive mood?

Healthy Activities: Going for a drive by yourself, sitting out in the sun, listening to your favorite music, watching your favorite movie, dancing, etc.?

Harmful Activities: Avoiding your family and friends, not eating, not eating healthy foods, staying in bed all day, not asking for help, etc.?

Healthy:

_____

_____

Harmful:

_____

_____

_____

_____

_____

Relaxation and Unwinding: Which activities help you to feel calm and relaxed? <u>Healthy Activities</u>: Taking a walk, doing a few deep breathing exercises, yoga, light stretching, meditating, listening to classical music, sipping tea, etc.?

<u>Harmful Activities</u>: Which activities make you more annoyed, frustrated, or upset... Drinking alcohol? Yelling? Pushing yourself too hard?

Healthy:

_____

_____

_____

_____

_____

Harmful:

_____

_____

_____

_____

_____

Resilience: What, or who helps you to bounce back from difficult times?

Healthy Activities: Maybe it's when you nurture yourself and cut yourself some slack? Or when you decide to embrace change? Reading books from your favorite mentor? Listening to a video or podcast?

Harmful Activities: What or who feeds your negativity?

Healthy:

_____

_____

_____

_____

_____

Harmful:

_____

_____

_____

_____

_____

Support Team: Which family members and friends can you count on to uplift and support you?

Healthy Activities: Who do you know that will allow you to simply feel the way that you feel, truly listen to you, and offer sound advice?

Harmful Activities: Who should you avoid during times of stress or crisis?

Healthy:

_____

_____

_____

_____

_____

Harmful:

_____

_____

_____

_____

_____

Final Thoughts

Dear busy mom,

As much as you love your kid(s), mothering is **hard**. It's something that requires you to constantly give and it's not always easy. May self-care be your guiding light, and something that will bring you calm and peace to your heart – even in the midst of chaos.

If you do nothing else than just give yourself permission to do something every day to feel good, that will be enough. Big or small, it doesn't matter. As long as it's something that will make your day a little easier and a bit brighter.

It's easy to be good to the kids, but make sure you're being good to yourself too.

Take time out of your busy day to just breathe, and be. You deserve it more than you know and you'll be a better parent for it tomorrow. Look at this new season as a renewal, there's a blank page before you. Create the version of yourself that you want to become. This is where your real journey starts. Enjoy the unfolding of it.

I really hope you enjoyed reading this book.

Wishing you the very best on your self-care journey through motherhood.

With love and gratitude,

Jody

P.S. If you loved the book, pass it on! Feel free to share with your online and offline mom groups, colleagues, family and friends. If you found yourself thinking about that one particular friend who could really use this book, tell her about it, send her the link or give her a copy as a gift. Feel free to share the love! ☺

More Resources

1.) If you haven't already…be sure to join our private Facebook Group of Moms!

   www.facebook.com/groups/mommyreboot

   We're passionate and determined to be a good mom by nurturing and taking care of ourselves. We're a supportive, loving, non-judgmental tribe lifting each other up and we'd LOVE to have you!

2.) If you're curious about coaching with me, I'm gifting you a free 45-minute sample session. Take the step. You'll gain powerful insight in this one session alone. There are no strings attached either. I do it because I'm grateful for you reading this book and I love connecting and helping others. You can schedule it here: https://calendly.com/jody11

3.) If you'd like to have me speak at your event, please email: jody@amommyreboot.com

   XoXo

   Jody

49494116R00159

Made in the USA
Columbia, SC
23 January 2019